Copyright 2014
Publisher: R. E. Stowell
Fairbanks, Alaska

I can do all things through Christ who strengthens me.
Philippians 4:13

Cover photo by Virginia Stevens. Photo of the author by Samantha Stowell. Thanks to Kara Stowell for proof reading, any remaining mistakes are my own.

All Rights reserved. Except for use in any review, the reproduction or utilization of this work in whole or in part in any form by any electronic, mechanical or other means, now known or hereafter invented, including xerography, photocopying and recording, or in any information storage or retrieval system, is forbidden without the written permission of the author or her heirs.

This is my point of view of my life, told from my perspective and totally my own opinion. It is not politically correct, nor is it prettied up to suit anyone else. If we learn from our mistakes, I should be just about the smartest person on earth.

Other books by Rosalyn Stowell
Don't Use A Chainsaw In The Kitchen – How-to and Cookbook
PAW (Post Apocalyptic World) Trilogy
The Beginning – Book 1
The Dark of Night – Book 2
The Dawn – Book 3
Alaskan Gold – novel, romance
Alaskan Alibi – novel, suspense
Stikine – novel, suspense
Cold Gold – novel, suspense
Klondike – novel, historical
A Head Of The Game – novel, serial killer
A Rat by any Other Name - novel

..And Then We Die
By
Rosalyn Stowell

My Dad's family moving to the Oregon coast in 1903

My Mother's Grandparents and Parents 1913

PART ONE – THE EARLY YEARS (BORING)

Chapter 1

This book is all about me. No dog mushing, no climbing mountains, no great drama nor any wonderful feats of courage. I wasn't even good at being a kid. Just an everyday life of someone that originally did not want to be in Alaska.

I have ridden on a sled pulled by dogs and it was fun, (thanks, Jean) I have climbed some steep hills, not much fun, and had a little bit of drama in my life, but nothing of importance to anyone but me.

As I sit here in my easy chair, relaxed, warm and well fed, I mull over my life and decide, all in all, it has mostly been a good life. If I could change a lot of it, I would jump at the chance, but then, would the end results have been the same? Besides, if there had been no Toad, I wouldn't have my two now-adult children. Hmm, my eye twitches just thinking about him, we'll get back to him later. No? So I look at the deep piles of snow out my window and think about my life.

I was born 9 months 2 weeks after Pearl Harbor. No mystery about why I was born. My father wanted to leave behind a male heir when he went off to fight. I didn't turn out to be male and he didn't get to go fight. He never quite forgave Uncle Sam or me. No good, try again. Two years later, Mom lost the twin boys she was carrying, try again……yeah, I don't remember any of that, but there are a few obscure memories.

Despite my father's fervent wish for a son, I wasn't. He never let me forget it. That set the tone for our relationship over the early years. Ignore me and I might disappear. Didn't happen. I have clear snippets of memory that are not from something I heard others mention nor did I overhear, later.

I remember being held by my Great Grandmother in a rocking chair outdoors. The only time I was around her, I was almost 3 years old, my mother was in the hospital and I was staying with my Grandmother. Later, when I was much older, I asked my Grandmother and she said she was making soap outside and brought out the rocking chair for her mother.

In my memory I am looking up at a very indistinct face surrounded by a halo of snow white hair with the sun directly behind her. I thought she was an Angel. She was soft, sweet and gave me a feeling of security and love.

Mary, the granddaughter a bit younger than me that Mom Miller was raising really didn't like having another little kid living there too, so bit me every chance she got. Our Grandmother was too busy to put up with this, so bit Mary to show her how it felt, then separated us by putting each one in a separate small woven wire fenced area around some small fruit trees she was starting. We were intent on murdering each other but the fences were far enough apart that only our fingertips touched.

When Mom Miller was done with her barn chores and came back to referee us, we were laughing together and touching fingers and remained friends the rest of Mary's short life.

After that, Mom Miller just stuck us in the old pig pen down the hill from the house so she could do everything needing done without chasing after a couple of two year olds or having us fall in the creek while she was busy.

Dad Miller was not around a lot as he worked in Oregon City at the paper mill. But when he was home, he woke us up in the morning, by singing. He had a wonderful deep voice and I loved listening to him. But after a while, if I didn't show up downstairs, he would ask if I was going to sleep all day, then quit singing.

Another snippet of memory is me being carried down a busy street and seeing a very large black lady with a wonderful smile. I thought she was wonderful and told her she was "Just simply gorgeous." She busted up laughing and hugged me. Told me no one had ever said that **to** her before. This was during World War II and the lady stepped back, but my mother laughed and told her I just said things as I saw them. I was 16 months old. All the way home, I tried to remember how to say the words that made the marvelous grownups laugh so much.

   My mother read a lot and held me on her lap while she read aloud, following the words with her finger. These were not children's books. She had no interest in children's stories, so I grew up knowing how to read and "Dick and Jane" were boring when I started school. I went through the library books every year, in grade school.

   If I misbehaved, I got a willow switch to the bare legs. That was to be avoided, so I behaved fairly well. My world was an adult world.

   Our house was in an orchard on a dairy farm, for my first 4 years of life. Mom would pitch rocks at the birds in the orchard, so I tried it one day on my way back in from the outhouse. I only found an old tin can, so threw that. It bounced back and tore my eyebrow in half over my left eye. I ran screaming into the house with my eye covered in blood and freaked out my mother. Eyebrows bleed, a lot.

   My Dad worked in the woods while we lived in that rental house in Mapleton. The Crummy would stop every morning and pick him up for work. His work was too important to the war effort to allow him to join the military which is what he wanted to do so bad he could taste it. There was usually one or two of the other loggers living with us and part of the time, one of Mom's sisters also would be living there to go to school. The school was located just across the highway from our home.

My Dad had been buying up the small homesteads up Ten Mile Creek, between Yachats and Florence for a while and decided to build up there and move us up. Mom was pregnant again after having lost the twins a couple of years before. Before she got to the point of not being able to do any of the heavy work, we would go up and work, during the day. Stacking rocks in the marked out foundation was something I could do.

There was no concrete used, just loose stack like the old fences used to be built. Every interior wall would have a rock foundation under it. We also built a huge rock foundation for the very large fireplace that would be the source of heat for the entire house. Another was built for the cook stove chimney. Both of these had a cleanout, under the house, plus supported the heavy stoves above.

Once the main floor was built, the fireplace was finished and was the only place to get in out of the rain. So I would play inside the fireplace while the adults worked on framing in the house.

I had a very loving early life as all the adults were very good to me. My Dad pretty much ignored me, but the rest made up for that.

Then my marvelous little brother was born and I adored him. Mom let me hold him and I folded all the diapers for her. When she had to start using a bottle for him as she couldn't continue nursing him, I was the one that checked to see if it was just right.

Then my Dad's oldest sister moved back from California and everything changed. She helped raise my Dad and he thought she was perfect. The first time I tried to do my job of folding the diapers for brother, she backhanded me across the room. She could not stand the sight of me and would hiss nasty things about me being a dirty German, to get away from her. (My Mother's Father was born in Vienna, Austria.) After that, I went to work on the job site with my folks or was dropped off at her mother's place a mile from our new home-to-be.

Dad decided we would go back to working on the new house and little brother would stay with the Aunt. Mom's doctor assured her the baby would be fine.

Aunt kept him for several months and he was not in very good shape when Mom got him back. Mom took him to the doctor and he bawled her out for treating a baby boy like that and she finally got mad as he was the one that encouraged her to let her dear sister-in-law raise the boy while the house was being built.

   Daddy and Aunt had been to an Attorney to see about them keeping the boy and kicking Mom and me out, claiming she was unfit to raise a child. He asked them about me staying with her then, they said I was old enough to manage okay. I was 4. After the deal with the doctor, they had to drop that idea.

   I was late getting back to the house just after we started spending nights one evening and it was getting dark. I took a shortcut through the piles of lumber waiting to be used on the house when the big stack of 2 x 10's for the rafters collapsed under me. I landed on my kneecap on the corner of a board with more landing on top of my knee. The pain was intense. Fifty years later, I had surgery to reattach my kneecap as it kept sliding over to the outside of my leg and letting my knee pop out of joint so I was never able to run. I seldom rush into things.

   The roof was mostly on and we were staying in the living room of the house. With no door on the house, only a large canvas tarp over the opening, when storms came up, the tarp would flap into the room. Waking up from a nightmare about getting eaten by a bear to have a huge cold wet tarp on you in the middle of the night is enough to make anyone scream, I thought. My folks weren't too thrilled about getting woke up that way, though. The screaming, not the tarp. It never hit on their side of the opening.

    I continued to have that same nightmare about the bear until just a few years ago. The Dream? My Mom, her youngest sister and I are walking down the hill from the grave beside the road toward our driveway. It is a cool day, and we are hurrying a bit. Suddenly a large black bear charges down the hill we are cutting across and grabs me from between them and carries me off. Over and over for over 60 years that damn bear got me. Once I started carrying a handgun all the time out here, my dream changed. The bear charged down the hill. I pulled the gun and shot him and that ended it.

    All the early years of living across the road from the school were at an end. I was going to start school, but school was 14 miles away and I had to ride in with the neighbor that lived a couple of miles beyond us. They owned an old military ambulance with benches along the sides, inside. No heat. They had two sons in school and my youngest Aunt also was still in school. She would tickle me until I peed my pants, then the rest of the ride was uneventful. I learned to not be ticklish, at all.

    Eight of the fourteen miles was on a single lane unimproved dirt road, just one step up from being a goat trail. At each mile post, there was a pull out. If you met another vehicle on the road, one of you backed to a pull out to allow the other to pass.

We moved into our house and Mom got her baby boy back. He was sickly and whiney, and she did not have time to cater to him like he was now used to. He cried most of the time. She had to hand spade a large garden area to plant for food, take care of chickens, rabbits and the milk cows we were given when we left the dairy farm. From being a spotless housekeeper in a home in town, she was now frazzled and overworked. Trying to raise enough food so we wouldn't starve and take care of a whiney baby didn't help. She hand washed all the laundry, including my Dad's work clothes. No time for housework now and the house was unfinished to boot. No finished walls, only the studs where walls would be someday.

My Dad started his own logging company and hired a couple of men to work for him. One was his nephew that lived 4 miles down the road from us. He still lived there with his Mom and Dad. Dad's older brothers still lived on the old home place three miles down the road. They had a nice orchard and guinea hens besides chickens. Those guinea hens were the best intruder alarms ever. No one went by on the road or stopped that they didn't let everyone know.

Mom was pregnant again and still having to do all the work Daddy considered woman's work. Anything to do with food or household was up to her. She was still doing the laundry on a scrub board in a wash tub set up outdoors near the creek. We hauled buckets of water from that creek for everything we needed water for, in the house. The outhouse was near the creek but farther downstream just in case.

This particular location on the properties Daddy had purchased happened to be his oldest brother's homestead. One of the old cabins was directly between where we dipped water and the outhouse. There were three of these cabins. My Uncle was not a housekeeper so when his cabin got too full to manage, he built a new one and moved over into it. He left everything in the one he moved out of, so each of the three cabins was chock full of interesting stuff.

Dad tore them down after my brother and I found a box of blasting caps and were running around shaking them as they rattled nicely. He probably should have looked through the cabins a bit better before burning as we all had to leave for a while when assorted ammunition started going off.

When Mom got close to time to deliver the baby, she moved to friends in Newport and stayed. I stayed with the lady that ran a grocery store, Bergman's, near the ocean, on coast highway 101. Our mail came there and the school bus stopped there every evening so we could pick up our mail on our way home. She was a sweet older lady and was very nice to me. She left me in the store one evening while she was pumping gas for a customer and I ate a candy bar from behind the counter. She was very upset and gave me a long lecture about stealing. I was crying because I was getting bawled out. I didn't even know it was stealing. That was my first and last candy bar for years.

Mom finally came home and I moved back home also. She had brought us a lovely dark haired girl and she was so little. Then the Aunt moved in with us to "help" out and I was never allowed around the baby again.

Once in a while my Grandmother would ride over on her horse. The girl she had been raising was now with her mother and stepdad and Mom Miller was now raising another granddaughter. When she rode over to visit, she put Dianne in her saddle bag hanging from the saddle horn. From the look on Dianne's face in the picture I have, she wasn't too happy about that, but then, she wasn't happy about a lot of things.

My Grandparents property on Ten Mile Creek.

Our house built on Ten Mile Creek.

Chapter 2

Dad owned just over a thousand acres of prime timber in the Siuslaw National Forest and they were not happy to surround us. For a while, there was a sign designating us as a Wildlife Refuge, also. No improvements were allowed on the road and getting a power or phone line up there was out of the question. We lived in Lane County, but went to school in Lincoln County as the closest school in Lane County was in Florence, but we actually somehow were listed in the Mapleton school district. No buses for that route.

Once the family left that used their ambulance as a bus, I would get dropped off at Bathurst Lodge across the highway from the beginning of Ten Mile Creek road and Daddy would give me a ride home after some drinks. Then the school district hired an independent contractor to bus everyone from me on up to Yachats. Bathurst Lodge had burned down.

One year, the new driver started checking lunches and keeping anything he liked. I brought a bag of Chitum berries to school and he took them, eating the entire bag full. We didn't see him for over a week and he never touched lunches again. Chitum is also known as cascara, the main ingredient in natural laxatives.

However, living in an area with very few neighbors and all but one couple were related, seemed pretty wonderful to me. The couple that were not family left every summer for their job on a forest service lookout tower.

From the day school let out in the spring, I was free. I could wander wherever I pleased and didn't really have any chores yet. Packing wood and water, mainly. The first couple of years before my brother started leaving the house too, were solitary and wonderful. It didn't matter if I dressed funny, couldn't run and had no idea how to make friends..

Once we were visiting somewhere and the lady disapprovingly chided my Mom for letting us run loose. "But what about the bears and other wild animals?" she asked. Mom just shrugged her shoulders and said, "They'll just have to look out for themselves, I can't keep the kids away from them all the time." We never went back there.

There were vine maple clumps on the hill above the house. They are far better than a jungle gym for playing and imagination. No matter how small the branches, they don't break. I could climb, jump, swing and play to my heart's content. The goats my folks let run were great for keeping the coast brush down under the trees so it was all open, like a park.

I don't know if these goats were descendants of the goats my Scots uncle brought to the coast at the turn of the century (1900) or not, but they ran wild and free. In the summer, that is pretty much what I did, too. Daddy got 18 cougar right around the house in the first two years we lived there.

Little brother was in trouble all the time. The Aunt had made little sister into a major tattletale. She rewarded her for telling on us, even if it was a repeat of things done a long time ago. I don't know how many times we got spanked for the same thing. So we started staying as far from them as we could manage. Lucky for us, the Aunt would go home once in a while, but she always came back.

Mom kept a kindling stick in the open wall sections of each and every room and that became the method of spanking us. No willows here, for switches.

About the time my brother started school, our Dad hired a man to operate the dozer on the logging operation. He had a sickly wife and 5 children. By this time, my Dad had bought out my Mom's folks across the valley a mile or so away and he moved this family into their old home. My Mom's folks moved over the hill to a place on the other side of Grizzly Ridge. Ten Mile Creek started on the west side of that hill and Indian Creek started on the other side. There was a very bad road over the hill and we would go visiting once in a while as it cut off a lot of travel to reach Mapleton, going that way. Grizzly Ridge was so named because legend has it that the last grizzly bear in Oregon was killed there. True? I don't know.

I didn't really have many daily chores except carrying water, firewood, feeding chickens and finding eggs, until the year my Mom got the measles. I was probably around 8 or 9 years old, school was out and as soon as Mom started getting sick, Daddy left. This left us with no way to contact anyone. People didn't drive up that road just for the fun of it.

We had 2 cows that were milking and the other animals, besides the garden to care for. I only knew how to cook French toast as long as the bread lasted, macaroni and cheese from scratch, no package meals then, and open a jar of peaches. I managed to keep the cows from drying up, but I had not milked before and learning on two heavy producers kept my hands sore for quite a while.

Mom was too sick to get out of bed, so I managed to keep us fed and the animals alive. No one wanted to eat mac and cheese for quite a while after she recovered. I started getting more chances to learn to cook, too.

Little sister was getting sick and we still didn't have any way to let anyone know we needed some help. Finally one of the loggers stopped by and we sent word with him. Somehow, Daddy got the word that his baby was sick, so he came home, picked up Mom and baby and took the baby to the doctor. She was not doing well as the measles didn't come out correctly on her and she was running a very high fever.

The nurse bawled Mom out for not bringing her in sooner and coming in public while her own measles were still visible under the skin a bit.

As far as I know, there were no social drinkers in the immediate family. There were drunks or teetotalers. I decided early on not to join the drunks. Coming home from school to find people passed out on the floor and under tables 2 or 3 days in a row doesn't give an enticing view of alcohol usage. Cleaning up the messes doesn't, either. Dodging grabby hands of inebriated geezers doesn't rank up there with things I want to do. Daddy said the difference between drunks and alcoholics is, "Us drunks don't have to attend those damn meetings."

A load of logs from our place. My Dad and one of his Jeeps. One of my Uncle's old cabins and his barn from his homestead.

My Grandmother, Aunt, Great-grandmother, Cousin and me.

Chapter 3

Every year at deer hunting season, we got to take time off from school and go hunting. Deer hunting was taken seriously by my parents. I was 2 weeks old the first time Mom took me hunting with her and we didn't miss any in the years after.

Usually Mom and I sang while we traveled, but not always. One year on our way home, my Dad finally had enough of my brother and I arguing, "Did not." "Did too" for about 500 miles and at the 499th mile, Dad broke. "If I hear another peep out of either one of you, you are going to walk home." It was late, heavy overcast, no such thing as street lights on a small dirt road, but did that stop me? No. After all, Daddy would never hear me. He was half deaf. One teeny tiny little "Peep."

On slammed the brakes, the door flew open, Daddy grabbed me by the scruff of the neck and out I went.

I was scared half to death and evidently little brother couldn't stop snickering as up ahead, the brake lights again blazed on and out tumbled my brother.

We were making pretty good time considering I couldn't run with my ruined knee and managed to keep the tail lights in sight up the twisty road. It had just stopped raining and as we neared home, the clouds started to part and a bit of moonlight shown down onto the wet road.

About a quarter mile from our driveway, was a sunken grave of one of the early day Homesteaders. As we passed the grave, the moon lit up the large dark mass slowly rising from the sunken grave, groaning "MooOOooo." At that point, ruined knee or not, Brother and I made it to the gate in time to open it for Daddy to drive on through going up to the house.

Our old black cow had been laying in the sunken grave and we startled her into slowly standing up, as we came rather loudly by, scaring each other with ghost stories about that grave. The moonlight on her wet hide gave her a shiny glow. Enough to scare us.

My Dad would take us out in the woods, walk us around and around a while, then ask us, "Where is north and where is home?" and we had to lead the way home. It probably helped us always find our way. My mind still asks "Which way is north?"

As the areas we camped and hunted got more crowded, Dad traveled farther and farther east and finally southeast while still remaining in Oregon. He enjoyed eastern Oregon so we started around Sisters,

Oregon and worked our way east and south and ended up down in the Steens Mountains, usually on the west side, but one year on the east side. For our access road at home and Daddy's logging, he always bought a small Willys Jeep. This was our only vehicle so it is what we all traveled in when we went hunting.

This was the days before lightweight camping gear, so we had a heavy duty canvas tent that shed rain as long as no one touched it from the inside, military type sleeping bags, enough food for 2 or 3 weeks, the rifles, hunting equipment and the 5 of us, all jammed into that small Jeep. One year we also had 2 young women from Canada that were visiting my Mom. Another year, we had the 2 oldest sons of the man Daddy hired to run dozer.

Then, when it was time to return home, we added the mule deer bucks gotten by my parents and later, my brother and I, also.

There was no sitting on a seat in the back. Gear was packed in behind the front seats until there was barely room for kids to scoot on their stomachs on top of the gear under the roof. The smallest one didn't want anyone to touch her, yet sprawled out in sleep and when she awoke, if anyone was touching her, she would started screaming. She tended to hide while we were in camp and not answer, so we spent a lot of time searching for her. She was just a little kid and didn't realize how scared we were that something had happened to her.

So after a couple of years of this, she had to stay behind at the Aunt's place, which did not sit well with her. Later, she got to come along with us again.

The year I was 12, the folks both got their deer the first morning we were there. That afternoon, we went on down to Fields for a nice drive and on a long open curve, Daddy stopped the Jeep, asked if I wanted to shoot the rifle and we got out. Over on the far side of the curve there was a small sage bush growing on the cut bank. Daddy handed me the 30-06, pointed at the bush and said "hit it."

I fired one shot, the bush vanished. He said that would do and we got back in the Jeep and went on to Fields. That was my firearms education and target practice.

Fields was a very small community. One building housed all the businesses and there were some private homes around the road going through the little town. One home belonged to the Magistrate and he also sold hunting licenses. I soon had my first hunting license and tag.

Each morning I would get up and carry the 30-06 out around in the sand dunes we were camped in and look for a deer.

Sand dune hunting is different than a lot of other types of hunting. Never go over the top of a sand dune, only walk around the bases and watch the brush on all sides. When a nice 3/2 mule deer buck and I met at the junction of some sand dunes, we were both surprised and my reflexes were young and good. One shot later, I had my first deer.

When I trudged back into camp, one of the fellows that lived there year around on his small ranch was visiting camp. I walked into camp, said "I got a buck." and sat down.

He looked at me and then at my folks and said "No, you can't have got a buck. You would be all excited and jumping around if you did."   I was too tired to do any jumping around or acting excited. I love eating venison so know I have to shoot them to do that, but I don't enjoy shooting them. Never have and doubt if I will start now. I have to look at them seeing roasts, steaks and burger, then I can shoot.

I took Daddy and the Jeep back to where the buck was located. Then the man believed I got a deer. A few years later, I watched him shoot a deer from the hill above and saw why he thought I didn't shoot one. I have never seen anyone get buck fever as bad as he had it.

The next year, when I was 13, we stayed at the ranch he was leasing. It had a large home on it and he had everyone stay in the house with him. He was a problem after my folks left to go hunting that morning and left us kids all asleep, by trying to get in my sleeping bag with me. I grabbed the top of the mummy bag and scooted to the bottom, hanging on for all I was worth. I about suffocated. He remained a problem for the next 4 years, whenever we went hunting and the one time he came and visited after we moved from the coast to a ranch in eastern Oregon.

He was always grabbing and touching, trying to catch me off guard. He grabbed me by the crotch, right in front of my parents one night as Mom and I were looking at magazines in the living room. They thought he patted my butt. His bed was the only place to sit, in there and we were laying on our stomachs reading. I kicked up and got him with both heels in the groin area. He hobbled around for a couple of days after that, but still kept at it. Later, Daddy wanted me to marry the man, telling me he was old and I would soon be a widow and own my own place. I was 15 at that time. The man lived to be almost 100 years old.

Mom and I took taxidermy lessons by mail, starting when I was 12. That was my main education for the artwork I do. We built all our own forms.

My brother fell and tore his underarm to the bone, exposing nerves and veins. Daddy was gone, Mom didn't know how to drive, no phone either, so she took off running down the road to try to find help.

My sister and I took brother to the creek and washed the sawdust and bar oil out of the wound. Mom finally found someone to come help, about 4 miles down the road. A logger our Dad disliked. He came back with Mom, they bundled up brother and took him to the hospital several towns away, leaving my sister and me at home. When Daddy got home near morning, Mom was back with brother, but Daddy was so mad that she accepted help from someone he hated, that he made her stand out in the rain to give them a check when they came by later that day on the road, on their way to work.

Mom learned to drive after that. So did I. I got to go along as she didn't back up and she didn't change tires or check oil. So I learned, also.

Daddy started taking us over to the area around Sisters, Oregon to camp for a couple of weeks each summer. It was beautiful there and he would drop us off to camp on Trout Creek near the base of the North Sister Mountain. One year, we also had my Grandmother and all 5 of the kids belonging to the man operating dozer for my Dad's logging outfit. We were all stuffed into the little Jeep with camping gear to stay two weeks.

Daddy had a new Jeep with a winch on the front one year, so drove and winched that Jeep to the top of the North Sister Mountain. I wonder if anyone wondered about tire tracks up there.

Evidently Daddy lost track of time and forgot to come get us one summer. The parents of the 5 extras didn't bring it up, either. Luckily, Mom had stuck a 25 pound bag of split peas in the load and we were reduced to split pea soup with no seasoning, 3 meals a day by the last week we were there. We hiked along the roads every day, for something to do as we had the area around camp thoroughly investigated. We found an old style log bear trap and tried to make it work again, we were hungry and would have eaten anything. We tried to catch fish by walking leg against leg and cornering a fish at the edge of the bank and scooping it out, but didn't work very well.

    A forest service truck stopped to see what we were doing and Mom asked about the distance in to Sisters as she was intending on walking in to get some groceries for us.

    The man was amazed we had been out there that long and that Mom was going to walk in for groceries. She refused his offer of a ride. Daddy showed up the next morning and was hauling us all to Sisters when we met the man in the forest service truck, bringing out a complete pickup load of food for us. He had a few choice words to Daddy which put him in a filthy mood for the rest of the day and all 8 of us kids stayed very quiet no matter who was getting crowded in the back of the Jeep.

    The next year when we went over for our camping trip, we snuck a rifle in under the load so we could get food if we were forgotten again. The year before, we could have devoured an entire deer or bear if given a chance and it was a while before any of us wanted to eat split peas again.

One memorable day at home, Daddy wasn't too pleased by his family. He called us all into the living room, lined us up, while he sat, spinning the cylinder of his little revolver, and told us he ought to shoot the lot of us and just start over. Then, several nights later, to wake up in the middle of the night to see him standing in our bedroom, just looking at us didn't add to the feeling of relaxation in the home. I held very still and pretended to still be sleeping. Not a restful night.

Dad's oldest brother went to Nome during the gold rush, then crossed the ice to Siberia because Nome was all staked already. He stayed in Siberia 2 years, dodging the Cossacks and mining. When he finally came home, he had enough that he never worked a regular job again the rest of his life.

He used to babysit us once in a while when we could escape from his sister's house and would put fur seal pelts on his bed for us to be on and dump a jar of nuggets for us to play 'marbles' with on rainy days, we lost a few through the cracks in his floor, he never got upset. If it wasn't raining, we would escape up over the huge sand dune behind his house and stay gone all day, roasting potatoes over small campfires and eating them hot and plain right from the fire. Burnt on one side, raw on the other. Yum.

He never spent much, lived alone in what most would consider a shack, but he was happy. He hunted, trapped a little bit, panned creeks for gold in the old Chinese workings along the Oregon coast and harvested wild plants to sell to nurseries and drug companies. Ferns and salal to florists, chitum bark and digitalis to drug companies. He would pay us to help him turn drying bark and chopping it to sell.

He didn't have a clue about kids, but we loved him. He always had patience with us. He gave me eyeballs out of a cow we were butchering because I was curious. I kept them in my pocket because they were neat, his sister snooped in my pocket while I was asleep, about broke my eardrums screaming when she found them. Rude awakening.

Having the five extra kids around all the time gave us someone to play with, if nothing else. Since they were around all day every day, Mom claimed she raised them but they did go home at night. The oldest boy considered himself too adult to play with us, and the next oldest thought he should be Boss as he was older than the rest of us We found an old barrel with the top cut out so decided to use it as a toy. We would roll it up the long slope of the hill the grave was on, near the house, then take turns getting in it and the rest pushing it off the hill and we would ride it down. The bossy kid decided he wanted to try it, so we stepped back and let him, after we had pushed it back up the hill. He rode it down and walked off. We pushed it back up, he ran up, pushing us out of the way and took another turn.

Uh-huh, we saw how this was going to work out. We pushed the barrel up the hill yet again and again he ran over, pushing everyone out of the way. This time when he started rolling, we were all on the other end, nudging the barrel to go to a certain spot, then stopped it and upended it open end down into a huge green grass cow pie.

Then we all took off to get out of sight before he managed to get turned back around and out of there. He spent the afternoon taking potshots at us with his .22 rifle, so we took the barrel to the large creek, cleaned it up and took it up the hill across the creek beyond the sawmill.

The donkey wasn't running to bring logs down from farther up and drop them over the edge of the large hill down onto the log deck for the mill, so we decided that would be the perfect hill to ride the barrel over. We were trying to decide who would get to go first when the two youngest boys said they should get to as both of them would fit in the barrel together. We finally agreed and they climbed in and we all donated our coats for padding as the day was warm and it was hard work getting that barrel up there.

We didn't even have to push the barrel, it took off on its own and dropped a bit over 10 feet before it hit the first time, then bounced and hit much farther down the hill and so on until it bounced completely over the log deck. Someone at the mill had noticed the barrel coming and they were all watching when it rolled to a stop out in the middle of the mill yard and two extremely dizzy little boys flopped out.

The rest of us disappeared during the barrel's trip down the hill as we finally figured out the boys might actually get hurt. The men had never seen the rest of us and the boys tried to say it was their idea and they took it over there, but they were only about 7 years old at the time and no one believed them. The rest of us were over at the house apologizing for killing the boys when the mill boss brought them home. We were all in some major trouble and the barrel disappeared, never to be seen by us again and the older boy got his rifle confiscated. He was the only one that mourned its loss.

Living near the Oregon coast had a lot in its favor. It is beautiful and green, year around. The trees are fantastic and almost anything will grow there, some needs protecting a bit, but it can still be done. Daddy traded it for a ranch in Eastern Oregon. Not one of the pretty areas, either. The ranch was a dry desolate looking place from my first view of it, in late December. We moved halfway through my senior year of high school a couple of days before Christmas.

I did not like change and hated having to move. I liked eastern Oregon to visit, but to move completely away from the coast and try to meet new people halfway through a school year? Not so much.

I was incredibly shy but determined that since no one knew me here, I could pretend I wasn't shy and try to make some friends. That actually worked!

My first deer, I was 12.

My 2nd deer when I was 13. My brother and sister with me on the tailgate of our hard top Jeep.

PART TWO - THE DUMBASS YEARS

Chapter 4

My first day of school at the new school I was scared half to death. I didn't know anyone. I had already taken most of the classes offered in this very small school. So I faked confidence.

It was the smallest public high school in the State of Oregon that year and alternated classes each year. One year, freshman/junior classes, the next year, sophomore/senior classes. I got there halfway through a freshman/junior year and needed 2 half credits in senior subjects to qualify to graduate.

There were eight of us in the senior class. Five girls and three boys. Even though I only needed two classes, I had to stay at school the entire day, so jobs were found for me to do. I pretty much put out the school newspaper and graded class papers for the teachers. I worked in the office part time, answering phones and typing up letters. The year was almost finished before anyone noticed I type using two fingers of each hand and my thumbs. No touch typing here. I do the same on computer keyboard.

I would read and memorize a paragraph and type it, watching the keyboard, managing to type 125 words a minute that way. I read very fast, so that worked for me. The teacher wasn't too pleased.

The new school was great. Everyone lived on ranches and had barn chores, so if anyone came to school with some odor lingering, no one paid any attention. No one was rich, so we all dressed about the same and I blended in.

By now, I was sewing fairly well, so made clothes for my sister and myself. We picked up bottles to sell along the roads and bought material. Flour sacks were patterned material, so we used a lot of those, also. My grandmother would buy material if I would sew clothing for her, and buy extra for me, for doing it. We were dressing better for school. I had a nice old treadle sewing machine.

The ranch Daddy traded the coast property for had several hundred head of cattle and some horses included in the deal. On the coast, we had all sat on the old donkey we had, but Jackie did not allow actual riding and when he got tired of someone sitting on him, we no longer were. He was very good at getting us off.

Now, we were expected to ride and herd cattle. Our coast cows came when we called and we could herd them on foot. These cows thought someone on foot was a target. Daddy bought most of our horses at the dog food factory. They were beautiful and young, so that ruled out the usual two reasons horses were taken there. No, they were there because of their personalities. I would have gladly returned some of them but actually, I do like horses. Catching some of them usually wasn't a problem, either. Staying ahead of them was much harder.

The hired man broke his leg soon after we got there and then it was just us. Daddy went back to the coast a while and we learned by doing to feed and care for cattle.

We learned to ride, with varying degrees of success. Sooner or later I was thrown from all but one of the horses we owned and one of the neighbor's horses, also. I was not one of the quick success stories. We did it though. We never lost a cow due to our not being able to ride.

We all rode. We doctored cows, we doctored each other. We all survived.

Dating was something I was not familiar with. I had gone on one date while still living on the coast and it was not a success by any standard. I seldom got to see a movie, so when I went on a double date to a drive-in movie. I watched the movie. My date was annoying me, so I put him on the floor and used him as a foot stool, until he agreed to watch the movie, also. Word gets around.

The new place was much better. No one had money, so we all went together in whatever car had enough gas to get us there and back. There wasn't really any separating into couples although most of the girls were engaged already.

We managed to go to all the Scots/American dances held within easy driving distance (100 miles) in the small towns around the area. Most of these towns had about 200 residents. The large town in the middle had about 1200 people and I think they counted strays and anyone passing through at the time of counting. There was one street light and it was a flashing red light. This was more my speed on being social.

I never had a curfew. However, if I straggled home at 5 a.m., I better be changed and have the tractor ready to go feed the herd after milking the barn cow for the house. There were no days off from those chores. The barn cow has to be milked at the same time, twice every day and the herd has to be fed once a day. No exceptions.

Two of the girls from school introduced me to their older brother and expected me to go out with him. He did show up in our car load of kids going to movies or dances, but was older and also smoked and drank. Somehow I just could not want to just go out with him. Then I learned he had just been released from jail on rape charges. Oh great. Not my idea of a good dating prospect.

I went to work in the cafeteria the fall after I graduated from High School. Daddy wouldn't let me drive to work, so after helping him feed the cattle in the morning, I would clean up, get dressed in my uniform, stuff the skirt under my belt and wear a pair of jeans to ride to work.

The horse I was allowed to ride to work was a nice enough horse, but he had been a full grown adult when he was caught up in the mountains and gelded, trained for riding and now I was using him as a taxi, into town even, and expecting him to behave?

He would shy away from every white spot in the center of the highway, then counter that by shying to the other side from the reflectors on the edge of the highway. So we traveled at a very erratic pace the 2 miles into town.

I tied his lead rope as I wasn't using a bridle, just a halter and one lead rope, in the yard of one of the teachers that lived at the bottom of the hill and ran up the hill, dragging my jeans down and my skirt out of my belt, trying to not trip myself and tossed the pants under the steps as I went through the large front doors of the school, hoped no one was looking as I ran through the halls to the cafeteria at the back of the building.

The two ladies that did the cooking would look at me, smile and shake their heads. I washed up at the sink and hurried to get everything ready to serve by the time the bell rang. I was never late, but sometimes it was a squeaker. Riding home was much faster and no shying from anything.

I managed to get hurt several times, getting bucked off from our lovely horses. Once landing on the back of my neck on frozen gravel, another time, also landing on the back of my neck and head on pavement.

The neighbor's horse that she wanted to show me, and decided we would ride double, was not happy to be ridden double, and bucked all the way across the highway. We reached softer ground and I told her I was jumping off and as I jumped, she decided to jump also and landed on her knees in my stomach. Then she stayed there, complaining about her knees. If I had managed to get any air in me, I might have hurt her.

I finally learned to stay on most of the horses. My own horse was a beautiful golden palomino mare. I painted a portrait of a neighbor's stallion in exchange for stud fees from his Appaloosa.

That Spring, I would take my soon-to-foal mare out along the highway right of way to eat the fresh early grass. I not only could ride, I was downright cocky about it. I would saddle her loosely and use only a halter to make it easier for her to eat. I would lie along her back, my head on her rump, my feet crossed under the saddle horn and read a book while she ate. We spent many pleasant hours this way, over several weeks.

One day she stuck her nose into a bush for a particularly nice bit of grass and found a roadkill rabbit. She shot straight into the air, I didn't fall off. My feet were stuck under the saddle horn. She bucked along the nice soft roadbed, up the driveway to the edge of the pavement. I finally got my feet loose and fell off over her head.

I landed on the back of my neck and top of my shoulders. Her front feet came down on either side of my face, pulling hair and pinching skin beside my ears. Her hind feet hit my backside and we went back down the driveway with me curled in a ball rolling under her big belly, being hit front and back by her legs. She never stepped on me the whole way down.

My grandmother was watering the front yard while this was happening. I don't know how much she saw of it, but as I lay there, still seeing stars, she asked me if I was okay. I gasped out "Sure, I'm fine." I couldn't move for several minutes.

There was a narrow road going up the butte across the valley from our house that led to our large middle pasture. We had to haul water up to tanks on top, every day. Daddy decided I should haul the water up. We had a 2 ½ ton flatbed dually truck with water tanks strapped in the back. This was a cabover type truck and I didn't even have a license to drive yet.

I drove the load up, unloaded into the tanks and drove back home all the time the cows were in that pasture, that summer. Mom followed me the last day we needed to haul water and about fainted. The road was so narrow, along the rim rocks that the outer wheel of the duals was out in midair most of the trip. Sometimes ignorance is bliss.

Another memorable trip with that truck, the tanks were out of the back and stock racks on. One of the cows had a problem we couldn't doctor at home, so Daddy told me to take her to the Vet. The Vet was located 2 small towns and at the start of the larger town away from the ranch. I still had no license. But, there was never a discussion about little things like that, if Daddy said do it, we did it.

I was making really good time on a long straight stretch when a State Trooper stopped me. He asked if I knew how fast I was going and as there wasn't a posted speed limit in those days, that was not a real problem. However, he suggested I drive a bit slower as the cow was about to have a heart attack, trying to brace herself with all 4 legs spraddled out to keep her balance. The truck would do 80.

Then he asked to see my license. I explained that I didn't have one, but Daddy told me to do it, so I was. He said he would speak to my Dad. He didn't give me a ticket. I think he knew my Dad. I never heard anything about it, but was not sent on any more errands on the highway driving that truck. I was old enough to get my license, but Daddy didn't want his insurance rates to go up with a teenaged driver.

After a few more close calls in other vehicles, Mom signed the papers for me to get my license and added me on the insurance. A week later, I was hit on the way home from a dance, by a drunk driver in my lane and practically severed my spine. No seat belts yet in those days, but if there had been, the car that hit me came down the inside of the driver's side, scraping the skin along the outside of my leg would have removed my legs.

As it was, I scooted over almost to the middle of the bench seat before he hit us. The surgeon wanted to fuse my spine solid. He said I would be totally bedridden by the time I was 30 if I didn't do the surgery. I did end up wearing a full body brace for a year after that accident. I was told I would need to wear it for life, but they didn't know me. I did, each time I was pregnant with one of my kids as my spine is not in good shape. When I am very tired, my back still twists sideways. But no surgery.

I think my Dad always figured kids and women were around to make life easier for guys. We did some of the hardest jobs, all learning on the job, of course. Haying, repairing equipment, moving cattle, branding them and doctoring them, we did it all.

One evening my sister and I were dressed to go to a dance, but decided to check a heifer one more time before leaving. Our father was drunk, so we couldn't depend on him to watch out for her. She had wandered from the area we thought she was in and it was dark by the time we found her. She had bogged down in an irrigation ditch, in labor, but had about given up.

She was half drowned and if we went for help, would probably not survive until we got back. My sister held the heifers' head up out of the water, I worked the calf's front feet free and started pulling. The heifer started giving some help and the calf came with a sudden whoosh of amniotic fluid. I landed on my rump in the ditch with the calf on top of me. The heifer knocked my sister back into the mud also, so we were both muddy and I was also bloody and gooey. Sis and I had to do some major cleanup before going to the dance.

The seeds from Foxtail grass work into the flesh under the tongue or in the throat of cattle, causing pus pockets to form. We would have to catch the animal, lance the infected lump and clean it out. With no anesthetic, they do not take kindly to this treatment. I can't blame them, but my brother, sister and I didn't get anesthetic for anything either, and were doctored the same way when we got sick or injured. Luckily we were all a sturdy lot and survived in spite of our self-doctoring. So did most of the animals.

When the first deer hunting season started, we were inundated with people that most of us didn't know. Friends of friends that knew someone had heard Daddy had a ranch in a prime deer hunting area. We had 56 people, all expecting us to drop everything and get them a deer. We had a lovely pile of firewood we had hauled in over the entire summer and they decided it was for them to enjoy huge bonfires. They burnt an entire winters worth of wood in a few nights.

Dad and Mom tried to be good hosts and we did all the work of feeding, and trying to find room to let them sleep. First one in a bed got the bed, so we never knew if we were going to find someone already asleep in our bed when we finished chores at night or not.

No one brought or bought groceries, no one gave a helping hand. It was a nightmare. We each got our deer and they tagged them, taking our tags off. By the time everyone left, our place looked like we had suffered a nasty bout of locusts. There was nothing left of the very large garden or our winter's meat.

Yes, we raised cattle. No, we didn't eat them. They were the profit and you don't eat the profit. I never cooked beef until I got married.

The next year, after an enforced winter of being vegetarians on low rations, we changed the rules. If anyone came back in the evening without hauling wood in, there was no bonfire and our stockpile was off limits. The first deer shot was the meat for meals until the next deer was shot. If they were slow filling their tags, the first deer was pretty much gone. Daddy still gave away our tagged deer to friends of his that didn't get a buck during season.

So Mom and I decided we were not spending another vegetarian winter. We knew the season was over. We really didn't care.

Daddy was furious the evening we came home from checking the back range for cattle missed during roundup. We unloaded my deer in the barn and he immediately started cutting it up for jerky. Mom snagged a few chunks before he got them cut in thin strips and we had some steak out of it. He ate the steaks and after that, we got a deer whenever we needed meat, but she and I took over the skinning, cutting and caring for the meat. He told us if we got caught, we would sit out our time as he would not pay a fine nor bail us out. We did share with some elderly folks around the area.

The sheriff knew someone was poaching deer in the area and we were the only new people, so he tried catching us at it. He set up roadblocks. We never were searched but the fellows let us right on through after looking at us through the windows. We always took a full change of quite nice clothes, including shoes with us. We always aimed for a neck shot. If it hit, the animal was dead, if it missed, it was a clean miss. One shot is difficult to place location.

After we skinned, gutted and loaded the animal, we took some of the coldest baths ever, depending on the weather but it was always cold. We would break the ice in a creek, strip off clothes and wash up, then put on the clean clothes we brought, including shoes. One drop of fresh blood on a shoestring would have landed us in jail. The meat, guns and dirty clothes were under the feed bags in the back of the Jeep.

Mom was on the coast visiting her family and Daddy was due home from the hospital from torn ligaments in the back of his thigh, when the Sheriff and County Appraiser stopped at the ranch to check out new buildings for improvements. The Sheriff thought he was going to find venison. He would have been right, but we could be sneaky kids. There was a whole frozen skinned out deer hanging in the smokehouse to the west of the main house.

They parked right in front of the house and we let them in, calm on the outside, panicked on the inside. We showed them our entire home, every nook and cranny as we tried to figure out what to do. Finally we could stall no longer. Little Sister and the spare girl (Linda) that was living with us took the men out the back door and headed east from the house, up the hill to the barn. Brother and I headed out the front door over to the smokehouse and got that deer down and back over into the house. The closest place to put it was in the parents' bedroom and the only place with room was in the bed but the deer was frozen solid, so it wouldn't make a mess and the blankets would insulate it to keep it frozen, right? After the most thorough inspection of the barn, the girls finally led the men back to the house and they went around the walkway out to inspect the smokehouse and oil house in the front. Success!

When they left, they pulled over across the road and watched the house for a long time. We went about our chores and ignored them. Daddy got home and sat in the living room a bit but was too tired to stay up and went to bed. The shriek he let out would have done any little girl proud. Then, as his foot hit the floor, he got a major cramp in the leg with the torn ligaments so he was hopping around in agony and we were trying to help him and get that deer out of the house.

It was fully dark by now and the Sheriff was long gone, so we hung it back in the smokehouse and Dad was finally able to sit back down after a quinine capsule and several glasses of water. Luckily for us, he had not been drinking on his way home, so he listened to our explanation and wasn't mad at us. After that, we cut up, canned and froze the deer as fast as we got them.

The next night, we kids went to a movie with the neighbor lady. When she dropped us off, my little finger got slammed in the hinge of the car door. It split the finger right down through the fingernail all the way down over both knuckles and was bleeding profusely. She told me to just go in and soak it in warm salt water and it would be fine.

I was wearing a pale lavender skirt with a white blouse and trying to keep from getting any blood on the outfit. Brother and Linda were checking the fridge and Sister went on up to bed. I stuck my hand in the sink full of warm salt water and instantly passed out from the pain. I evidently slid down the hot water heater and my hand flopped onto my chest. My head was still held up by the tank, so my breathing sounded terrible. Linda pushed open the door and my head banged back on the floor so finally some air was getting through, but all she saw was all the blood pouring over my white blouse and skirt. She started shrieking.

Brother was trying to catch her to shut her up, and Daddy woke up to pandemonium in the other room, jumped out of bed, landing on that same injured leg which went into spasms. By now I finally had enough air to regain consciousness. Linda was still shrieking, Daddy was howling in pain, Brother was yelling at Linda to shut up, Sister was peeking around the stairway door trying to see what the problem was.

I tightly wrapped a washcloth around my finger and held pressure to slow the bleeding and stepped out in front of Linda on one of her trips around that center table. Brother held onto her with a hand over her mouth, Sister and I got Daddy another quinine capsule and water and back into bed. We cleaned up my mess and all went to bed after I wrapped my finger in gauze and taped it.

If Daddy had been drinking, there was no discussing anything with him. One night Brother and I had gotten home just before Daddy did and when he came in, he decided to cook some steaks we now kept ready, in the fridge. We offered to help, but he said he would do it himself. He got out a skillet, poured cooking oil in it, put some steaks in it, watched them a few minutes, turned and seasoned them, then sat down and ate them. Brother and I never said a word, but the stove was never turned on the entire time and we headed up to bed rather than get ourselves in trouble by saying anything or laughing.

I moved down to the other main house not long after to live with my Grandmother. That was a very nice time for me and in the evenings, I would read a short story by O. Henry out loud to her as she sat in her rocking chair near the heater. Muumuus were popular then, and she loved them, so I started making them for her. She bought some of the prettiest brilliant material and loved the bright dresses. One of her daughters was a fine seamstress but always made dark clothes for her that she wore but didn't care for. She liked colorful and that is what I made for her or later, bought, the rest of her life.

One family living near us were Klamath-Modoc and French. The kids were about the same ages we were and they had lots of cousins. Even though some of us (me) were of the ripe old age of nineteen, we still played cowboys and Indians on horseback. The slight twist to this was, the Indians usually played the cowboy parts.

Several other kids would join in and we would ride like banshees over the hills. We certainly livened up several tourists' vacations and one new family moving into the area from the east coast. They had been expecting wild Indians from the time they crossed the Mississippi. There were about 40 of us the day they thought they were under attack. We didn't even know they were there, until we saw some silly people dressed in suits and dresses diving for the bushes and the full irrigation ditch. What a first impression we made on each other. I haven't changed mine, of them.

One evening Daddy was three sheets to the wind and started in on me again about only being a girl and it was Mom's fault. Having learned in school that the male determines the sex of the child, I had to inform him of his mistake. I was so lucky he was as drunk as he was, because if he had ever connected with any of his roundhouse swings, he would have torn my head off. (He used to bareknuckle box, for fun.) We were making laps around the kitchen table with an elderly friend looked through the door and saw what was happening. On one of Dad's swings as I was close to the door, he reached through, grabbed me and yanked me outside, leaving Daddy looking around for a target. He gave me a ride to the dance they were holding that night in the little town 2 miles from the ranch. I never heard any more about it being Mom's fault, though.

My Grandmother and I

Chapter 5

Mom was in the hospital a few days and somehow made friends with a woman from Italy that was also there, having just had preemie twin girls.

Mom didn't speak Italian and Tony didn't speak English, but they became great friends in a couple of days and Mom volunteered me to move in with Tony, in town, as she was leaving her in-laws ranch where they made her and her 2 year old son live in a line shack out across a field they refused to let her drive her car across. She not only had to carry all the food and water used, but her son also, while pregnant with the twins across a fence and through a large hayfield, then over another fence. Later, her husband just couldn't believe she would leave him and get a divorce. He was military and gone overseas all the time.

One of the nurses found her a small cheap cabin to rent and someone else found her a job washing dishes in a café. Mom gave her me, to take care of the 2 year old son and the newborn twin girls. The girls were so tiny their arms were the size of my little finger and I was scared to death I would damage one.

I had never babysat for anyone and folding diapers for my brother when I was 4 did not count much, now. Tony was from a wealthy family in Italy, grew up with nannies and her idea of how a perfect mother acted was, she kissed them all goodnight and said a prayer over them, then left. Her husband had always hired household help for her, before he left her to the tender mercies of his family on their ranch. She didn't know how to cook or do housework. This was a whole new life and she was overwhelmed but willing to learn.

She left for work as soon as she woke up in the morning and stayed gone all day. I didn't have a clue what I was doing.

The tiny house we lived in was two very small rooms and a miniature bathroom. The bedroom had a double bed crammed in it that she and I shared and two cribs stuffed between the wall and the foot of the bed. We had to climb on the bed to reach either crib. The twins were in one and the boy in the other. The front room had a couch, small table, 2 chairs and a small counter, sink and the smallest stove to cook on that I have ever seen. There was no source of heat. We would have frozen in the winter.

One of Daddy's acquaintances broke in the front door and tried to assault me. I was putting up a heck of a fight but he was loving that, so I went limp. He thought I was giving in and relaxed his hold on me. I bolted and got around the table, he went over the table to grab me again. Having just done dishes, I knew where I always put the large butcher knife. I grabbed the knife and whirled around just as he grabbed me again but now the knife was against his pot belly.

He started saying I wouldn't dare, he knew my father. Well, Whoopty-doo. He yanked me toward him and I let the knife stay between us, not even giving it a shove as it was very sharp. The point sank through his shirt and disappeared into the pot belly a couple of inches. The sight of his own blood cooled off his ardor immediately and suddenly he was screaming at me that I was crazy and he was going to see me institutionalized. I'm still waiting. He finished ruining the table and right on through the front door. He may have needed a band aid, but wasn't hurt much. He died years later from prostate cancer. No, I had nothing to do with it and didn't use a voodoo doll, either.

I am still amazed the babies survived and so did the 2 year old. I stayed with her a year. We did move to a larger house and that helped a lot. No pay, no time off. She finally remarried a nice older man that thought she was perfect and loved the kids. I went back to the ranch.

Our ranch house and yard

The tractor I learned to operate so I could quit the pitchfork on the haystack.

Chapter 6

Then I started driving for a blind guy. His uncle needed a ride back to San Francisco to go back to work on an oil tanker. He had spent his holiday up visiting family. So from driving in a town with one stop light, I now drove down to San Francisco. Talk about culture shock. We drove into town on a Friday evening when I think the whole town migrates to Nevada. The posted speed limit was 70 mph at that time, but if you only went 70, you got ran over. Wall to wall headlights coming at me.

We ended up staying in San Francisco for Halloween and that was an eye popping event. This was in the very early 1960's so I had no clue grown-ups acted that way or dressed that way, for that matter.

I got to see a lot of the sights, Fisherman's Wharf, Alcatraz from a distance, Chinatown and to drive down one of the worst streets imaginable for someone not used to even traffic lights other than red. That street gets a lot of exposure in assorted movies.

The blind guy got possessive and the cowboy fellow from my early teen years showed up at my parents' ranch, expecting me to marry him. I was in a hurry, as I wanted to get the blind guy home and return the car he provided, I was quitting.

The cowboy was not a large man and I had spent the summer bucking bales and moving cows, so when he stepped in front of me and demanded a kiss to let me pass, I put my hands along his sides, picked him up and moved him out of the way. Talk about messing up a man's ego. I didn't know they were so fragile until years later. Sheesh.

Money was a scarce commodity for all the students, so whenever there was a dance or movie, most of the Senior class could fit in one car and attend. I had never done any of these things before and loved it. I didn't have a clue about relationships or what to look for in a husband.

If Home Ec was supposed to help teach girls homemaking skills and what to look for in a husband, I must have been absent the day they covered telling toads from frogs. I had a vague idea of being a rancher's wife and caring for the house and some children in the dim future maybe, but not for a few years after getting married. Ha.

I met the Toad while he was working at a feed store in Canyon City. I didn't know he was only there as a favor to a friend and that actual WORK was a dirty 4 letter word to him. We dated, sort of.

My brother and friends always went along with us. I didn't know to find out the important things, like what he expected us to do in the future and how income would be handled. I thought the man of the house paid all the bills and handled that stuff.

I would have been a great 1950's prototype housewife. Unfortunately, this was the early 1960's and things were not the same.

I should have been suspicious when his parents were sweetness and light about loaning him their car so we could go out. They were always violently opposed to loaning it for any other reason. They also remained on their best behavior with only a couple of lapses into the usual screaming matches I found prevailed any other time.

Somehow, they decided that since I was the oldest child of my Dad's, that when I married, they would be on easy street. My parent's ranch had been two ranches at one time and still had two complete headquarters, a nice ranch house with barns and corrals at each. There were numerous small houses and bunk houses, also. They planned on moving into the other main house. That family did a lot of wishful thinking, then thought it was reality.

As soon as the word "Yes" escaped from my mouth after he asked me to marry him, I wanted to yank it back. He asked his brother if he heard me say yes, then told me he would sue for breach of promise if I reneged. He laughed as though that was a joke, but the look in his eyes said he meant it. His parents immediately hauled us over to Idaho where there was no waiting period and got us married. Well that wasn't exactly what I pictured for my wedding.

I did my best to be a dutiful wife. Obedient, loving and kind. Then I found out my husband was, in reality, a Toad. It's not that he was cold blooded, just that he started looking and acting like a Toad.

We moved into a small apartment over the bakery. I loved the smell but they started work right under our bedroom at 3 a.m. I am a very light sleeper. Then I had to get the Toad awake in time to go to work at the mill he had just started working in. That job lasted almost 3 months and ended up being a record for longevity for a few years. Then we got evicted as he was not paying the rent and as I packed boxes to move, I found all the bills stuck behind the desk.

Being too stubborn to admit a mistake, I kept trying to treat him the way I wanted treated so he would become the loving, kind prince that would love and care for me and our future children and we would live happily ever after. He took it as his due and only got worse.

Shortly after that, I found out I was pregnant. I had continued having periods so I was already four months along before I knew I was anything but sick. He came in drunk and took a swing at me. Oh hell no. I sat up all night, waiting for him to wake up and be sober enough he would not be able to use being drunk and not remembering as an excuse.

He puked all over himself and the bed and I was not about to sleep near or with that or him. I had his extremely sharp small ax he practiced throwing in my hand and was thwacking it into the other hand when he woke up and started complaining because I hadn't cleaned up the pukey mess like his mamma always did. "Well, first off, I'm not your momma. Second, if you ever swing at me or hit me again, I will fix you. Since you are bigger than me, I will have to use an equalizer and you won't be able to sleep or turn your back, because as soon as you do, I WILL get even."

He had been around ranches enough to know what getting fixed meant. Even after we separated and he broke in the door to my apartment, intent on beating me, he managed to talk himself out of it. He had my shirt front and some of me in one fist and my feet were dangling near the floor, his other fist drawn back to smack me in the face. When I am scared to death, I start giggling or laughing and I was thinking in my head, "Shut up, he's going to kill you, fool."

Then he started his own argument. "You want me to hit you, you'll call the police on me and get me arrested. You know you will be believed and I will be blamed." Well, yeah, since he wouldn't have a mark on him and I would be knocked out and bloody with my door kicked in, probably. He dropped me and ran back out of the room. He took the kids and left State right after that. But that is way ahead of my story.

My folks let us move into one of the small cabins across the main highway from their house. It didn't have a roof, insulation, electricity, running water or sewer, but it had walls and a floor. We fixed the roof. Mornings, I would pass out between the house and the outhouse, no one noticed. I eventually always came to and went back in the house. Pregnancy was rough. Mom told me she would not babysit, ever. She never did, either.

His parents came down and asked to buy a beef from my folks and they butchered one out for them. They took it home. The next year, they were back asking for another beef and my Dad held out his hand and said when the last one is paid for. They mentioned the other house as it was vacant at the time, Daddy said if he wouldn't let me move into it, why did they think he would let them move in?

They started not being as nice to me. In fact, they started treating me like slave labor. I was very pregnant by this time, so they figured I would never leave and would put up with anything. His youngest brother asked why he treated me like that, he told him he didn't HAVE to be nice to me now, we were married. Later, the brother offered to take care of the problem for me, I would have let him, but I liked the young man and he was too nice a person for that.

We moved back up near them and the Toad went back to hanging out with his ex-girlfriend, the one he went to school with, Dorothy. I got dumped at his parent's house every evening.

I was morning sick 24/7. I puked until blood spattered most of the time. I weighed 145 pounds when I got pregnant, I weighed 142 pounds when I went in to give birth. I'm 5'8" and had been quite muscular. I could keep sour green apples and jerky down. The smell of Bay Rum aftershave will still make me hurk.

I finally got a decent settlement from the car accident involving the drunk driver. I prepaid the hospital and doctor for the upcoming birth, and banked the rest. There was an adorable house, barn and 15 acres for sale a few miles out of town and I really wanted it. This settlement would cover the entire purchase.

The next night, the Toad drove home in an institution green car belching smoke and no working heater. He was on his way to the custom car shop to get it tricked out. A very pricey metallic blue paint job, matching tuck and roll leather interior, seats, headliner, carpet, it was beautiful to look at. The oil was still pouring through it and the heater still didn't work, but the entire insurance settlement was right there, in that damn car. He told me if I hadn't of been so stupid as to prepay the hospital, there would have been enough money to fix the heater and the motor, too.

    I wasn't due for another 2 weeks, so we went out to load baled hay to feed cattle and maybe get a deer to feed us. The Toad's family would sneak into the rock cellar behind our house and steal food. I finally placed my childhood collection of assorted eyeballs, rattlesnakes and embryos preserved in alcohol or formaldehyde around through the other canned goods. Some of them came up missing and after that, no more food was stolen and they never ate at our house again, ever. But now we were out of food and needed a deer.

    This was February, so not exactly legal season. My brother-in-law was driving the old farm truck. I was sitting in the middle and the Toad was by the other door. We spotted a herd of deer on the other side of the field and headed over to intercept them. He saw the deer alright, but did not see the large dry irrigation ditch across the field and we hit it quite firmly.

    My head hit the ceiling and everything behind the seat had bounced up, also, so instead of coming down on the seat, I was pinned up in the air with the gun jammed into my belly and the jack behind the thin seat in the middle of my back.

He got the truck stopped on the other side of the ditch finally, and he and the Toad had to lift me up in the air to get the jack to drop behind the seat and pry me off the gun barrel. We drove on out to the haystack and loaded the large truck full of baled hay. The deer were long gone.

That night, as soon as I relaxed in bed, WHAM. Labor started hard core. My pains started at 5 minutes apart. Toad was already asleep, I got up and washed my hair and almost drowned myself when a contraction hit while my head was under the faucet in the tub. I cleaned house and did the dishes as I was told first labor would take many hours. When the pains were 1 ½ minutes apart, I woke the Toad to drive me to the hospital. He mumbled it wasn't time and went back to sleep. I did a few more odds and ends around the house and finally told him I was going, with or without him, the pains were less than a minute apart. He grumbled and whined the whole way, but did take me.

I walked into the private hospital that was the only hospital available for a couple hundred miles and the nurse on duty asked why I was there at 5 a.m. I told her I was in labor and she laughed and said sure you are.

I carried the baby very low and was wearing a full skirt with a cinch belt that hid what little tummy I had. However when I doubled over, she at least let me sit down and then the other nurse came in that was on duty, and they undressed me and finally could see that indeed I was pregnant. The baby looked like just some skin draped over her as she laid curled by my pelvic bone.

When they examined me, they called the doctor. There was another doctor visiting from England that eventually moved there and went into practice and he came, too. He wanted to do a C section as the baby was not turned and they did nothing to turn her the correct direction. She ended up being born butt first.

All natural childbirth was my doctor's idea and she would not budge on it, no matter how the birth was proceeding. I got to listen to them discussing whether or not they would save the mother or the baby when I started hemorrhaging. They had me strapped down or I would have gone home about then.

She weighed 7 pounds, 12 ounces and was almost 19 inches long with a large bruise on her lower lip from the gun barrel. I had massive bruising on my back and stomach. The nurse that hopped up on the table and almost smothered me while pushing down on my belly may have got scars from me biting her thigh so I could get some air. She was the only one that screamed that day. Screaming tightens the wrong muscles and makes it hurt worse.

The Toad and his buddies spent their days hunting ground squirrels for a rancher near town.

He supplied their ammunition, sodas, tobacco and meals. They were happy. The baby and I were pretty much on starvation diets. I could no longer nurse her as my milk now looked like water. I had a bag of macaroni, no cheese and a bag of plain oatmeal in the house. That was it. Not even salt.

Mom stopped to visit and noon passed without me fixing anything for lunch. Finally she asked and I started bawling. We lived just across the street in the old sheriff's office from the grocery store in front of a defunct brewery. The back room of the sheriff's office had a secret door into the brewery. This was all closed down, but the 500 gallon vats and all the tools were still stored in the huge dark old building. Mom bought a very large supply of food for me and the baby and we stashed it in the brewery. She did not want the Toad to get one mouthful of it.

By this time, I had miscarried a child and was pregnant with another as the doctor had told my husband that to get me over any fear of giving birth the best thing would be to make sure I got pregnant immediately, which he set out to see to. I did not have a say in this. Getting woke up during the night being screwed isn't fun.

The rent on the sheriff's office was $10 a month and we got evicted because of nonpayment of rent. I was sadly disillusioned with my husband by this time and if I had known anything about welfare or any other program to help out, I would have been gone.

One year our total cash income was $236.00 and I kept the tax return as evidence.

Daddy had told me when I got married I was not welcome to move home or back on the ranch by myself. I didn't know how I could support my daughter and unborn child, so I stuck it out. Besides, marriage was for life. This was looking like a very long, hard sentence.

We went to Eugene, Oregon. The Toad's oldest sister and her husband and family lived there. They owned a small store and lived in the back of it. They were crowded, we added to that. They placed a folding cot in the hallway between their children's bedroom and the bathroom, so everyone using the bathroom had to sidle past us. The Toad was well on his way over 300 pounds by this time and he took the wall side, so no one would bump him and disturb his sleep. I got to perch on the side rail and hang my pregnant belly out over the side. The little travel bed was set at the foot of our cot for the baby.

Luckily for me, their kids loved the baby and would be as careful as possible to not disturb her if she was sleeping and play with her if she was awake. They were really good kids. Their stepfather was another grabby, obnoxious person and everything said had a double meaning. He looked for reasons and excuses to push against, rub all over and generally make himself odious. He made sure to let me know if I complained to his wife that I would be out on the streets.

The Toad actually got a good paying job. We found a house to rent and the week this baby was due, we went back over to Canyon City to pack up our stuff and move. Toad's parents had given away our car with my saddle, all the tools and assorted stuff still in it. His older brother drove it until it ran out of oil on the freeway and walked off and left it sit there. Nothing was removed from it and it had a 5 gallon can of oil in the back. Yeah, it was still an oil burner.

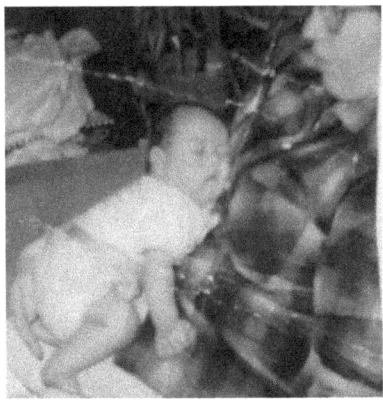

My daughter and I

View from the ranch house

View continued

Swimming hole, South Fork John Day River

Chapter 7

Our move to Eugene was made on the night the baby was due. A friend volunteered to use his pickup and haul our furniture over for us. So, since he was a friend and shouldn't have to make the trip by himself, the Toad rode with him and I drove the station wagon we now owned. All our clothes, dishes, bedding, mattress, the baby and I were stuffed into it. This new baby was carried very high and trying to fit behind the steering wheel was a chore.

The roads going over the Cascade Mountains near the end of March were not the best and we hit a lot of rain, ice and fog. I had to stop almost every rest stop for the bathroom and got yelled at for slowing the trip down. Like this is where I wanted to be.

Our new home had a reason for being so cheap. It was located in the edge of the railroad yards and the noisiest place I have ever lived. This baby was making up for the first one being 2 weeks early and came 2 weeks late. Since I didn't even have a doctor here and had not seen one the entire pregnancy, the hospital was not pleased with me when I showed up very early one morning in labor.   This was a very large hospital, especially compared to the little private one my daughter was born in. Sacred Heart is a teaching hospital.

The way it is supposed to work, you get on a trolley table on a rail up at the top of a sloping corridor that curves down into the amphitheater where a gazillion people sit around above you and get to watch you pop out the kid. There is no privacy and you are on display.

When they finally decided it was time for me to walk down the hall to that set-up, I was more than ready to get this over with. They had given me a shot when I arrived that allowed me to sleep between contractions and I wasn't totally worn out.

We passed a pay phone in the hallway at 8 a.m. and they asked if I would like to stop and call my husband to let him know I was going in for delivery. I was feeling an urgency they were not and said no, just point me where I need to go. I speeded up and made it through the swinging doors and onto the trolley. The doctor rushed in right behind me and was yelling "wait a minute." Out popped the kid and he caught him like a football, right in the numbers. Luckily, he didn't fumble. Time of birth, 8:06 a.m.

Being born that fast isn't actually all that good for the baby. His lungs collapsed. They kept him crying and got him into an incubator which really didn't fit too well as he was 9 pounds and 23 inches tall. I got to go home the next day, he had to stay a week.

Toad found another house to rent as the trains were keeping even him awake and we made another middle of the night move. Now with computers, this would not have been so easy to manage. He still didn't pay the bills but that didn't mean I was supposed to, either. I got just enough money to buy groceries.

He still went out evenings and had a girlfriend here named Ginny. We had now been married two years and had two children 13 months apart. I knew whenever he saw a girlfriend as he would always come in the door yelling at me for running around on him. Yes, I had two small children, no car and no phone, I was really out running around with other men. I had one, why would I want another one? At this point, they seemed vastly over rated.

I did get a part time evening job, inking in cartoons for an artist named George Cochran. He also painted people and paid me to pose for him. I earned enough to keep the kids well fed and dressed decently. He also taught me how to do lampblack paintings. He was Cherokee and said he learned the process in a dream one night. It is similar to charcoal painting, but a much softer finished product. It is powder and used dry with a brush. I still do those once in a while. The Toad actually got me the job.

Then the Toad got hooked on a TV series, "Dark Shadows". He managed a call out every afternoon so he could drive the service truck home and watch his program. For some reason, his boss wasn't that thrilled with this new interest.

So now he lined up another job up at Mill City. We were living in another house farther out of town by this time so it was a simple matter for him to just tell me we were moving and we were gone before morning.

A couple of months later, we moved from Mill City to Redmond, Oregon. This was the first place I ever bought a chicken to cook and it was hairy. So I used rolled newspaper and a fork and burned the hair off each piece. The Landlord came over to see what I was doing and I told him I was BBQing chicken, very rare.

The Toad lasted on the job there almost two months. Then we were homeless again and my parents let us move into the other large house on the ranch. So back to Dayville, for us.

Toad and I went to a movie one evening, and when we came home, the house was ablaze with lights, the yard full of cars. The babysitter was throwing a party. They left fast after we got home, but the house and yard were trashed. We told them we wouldn't tell if they came back the next day and cleaned it all up. They didn't, instead they drove by throwing things down at the house and killed our little dog. We turned them in to the police.

They all turned up in Court with an attitude right up until the tape recorder was turned on. They had used our reel to reel tape recorder and recorded most of the party.

The Toad got a job at the mill up at Bates and made a deal with someone in Prairie City to rent a house in exchange for repairing it. The house was a nice house and I worked on fixing it up as we lived in it. The terms were not written down, so the day the owner checked in and it was done to his standard, we got evicted as he had a paying renter lined up.

A rancher just west of town allowed us to move into the small apartment over his garage. It was extremely crowded as they stored old furniture and stuff in it also. Then my brother, his pregnant wife and her sister showed up wanting to move in with us. They stayed overnight and decided it was too crowded even for them.

The rancher had a nice larger house needing a lot of work, so made another deal, repair the house for rent. He would supply all the needed supplies as the person living in it before had knocked out most of the windows, kicked panels out of doors and tied a dog to each door and never let them outside. What a mess. The plumbing had frozen up, also, so it all had to be replaced.

The Toad worked at the mill and when he was done at the end of the day, he went and played, so he wasn't going to be doing any of these repairs. He didn't on the other house, either. However, I was learning a great deal. His main girlfriend here was his friend Dwight's sister-in-law.

I replaced the glass in 23 windows of this house. That part was easy as the man at the hardware store described how to do it. The plumbing was harder. I had never repaired plumbing of any sort. The 14 year old son of a friend with 12 children and the 90 year old neighbor man came over to see if they could assist. The Toad even accused me of fooling around with those two.

The boy didn't mind crawling under tight spaces and he and I did the wrench work while the elderly gentleman stayed on his horse and told us how to do the work. That man kept that horse saddled and tied by the door all day every day and never walked anywhere.

He drank every Saturday night and the horse that was so feisty during the day was a very patient caretaker at night, bringing his person home.

During the day, the horse shied at everything and a major job getting him to cross bridges or around the cattle guard by our driveway. However, once the old man was soused, the horse leaned against the light post with spikes up it for steps so the old man could climb on. Someone turned on the light hanging from the horse's tail and he slowly started for home. He walked sedately over both bridges and tiptoed over the cattle guard by our house. When he got to their house, he leaned against the porch railing and the old man would slide off and go in the house and to bed. The horse let himself into the barn lot and stayed until someone came out and unsaddled him.

Thanks to this kind elderly man and the young boy, the house was finally ready to move into. Not for most folks, but we did anyway. I had scrubbed the floors until no sign of the dog mess remained. The windows were all in, the plumbing worked. I could do the rest while we lived in it.

I replaced the interior doors, painted all the walls and started fixing the floors. When the back door was shut, snow drifted in under it. When it was open, it snagged up on the floor. The young boy and I were jacking up the corners and replacing support blocking under the house.

Then the Toad got fired and we again were moving in the middle of the night, although we didn't owe back rent here. However, we were leaving before the job was finished on repairing the house.

We moved to Mt. Vernon. Toad got a job as night watchman for the burned out mill there.

Salmon were running in the river below the mill, so the Toad and a friend decided to catch some to smoke. They tied a bundle of dynamite together, stuck a cap in it and some fuse and headed over the bank to catch some fish. They went up the gravel bar to the head of a large pool in the river and pitched the bundle of dynamite as far out as they could, then came running back down the gravel bar. I was up on the bank above them and tried to get their attention to the fact that the dynamite was drifting down the river, right beside them.

I yelled, screamed, waved my arms and they laughed and waved back, thinking I was enjoying this, too. Then the fuse ran out and the entire river whooshed up in a geyser showing bare river bed on both sides of it and knocking both men flat on the ground. Bits of fish floated around and we quickly headed back to the office and pretended we had been there all the time when people showed up trying to find the source of the large explosion. No fish for us.

While using the wringer washer, a sheet got stuck in the wringer and put too much pressure on it, exploding the whole thing into my face. This broke off my two front teeth and the pain was excruciating. The new dentist in John Day worked me in and pulled my teeth. All my upper teeth.

I got home to find the Toad had got me a job cooking at the café across the highway from our house and I was late.

I walked across the street to get yelled at and I mumbled an apology through the bloody gauze pads in my mouth. The man finally took a look at me and got a little red faced. He made sure I stayed in the back that shift so no one could see what I looked like as I spit blood all through the shift. That's really what a customer wants to see fixing his dinner.

The Toad reasoned that since my shifts cooking was during the day and his shift as night watchman was at night, we would be making a lot of money and he would take care of the kids during my shift. That lasted one whole shift and before the end of it, he walked the kids across the street and sat with them in a booth through the rest of my shift.

Then he hired the daughter of the breakfast cook to babysit which pretty much used all I made per shift just to pay her. Yeah, that made sense.

We were down at my parents place during a weekend off when a lady my family had known for years stopped by with her new husband. They were living in Alaska now. Since that was a few thousand miles away and on an island to boot, they felt safe offering us a place to stay if we were ever in the area.

Poor dears. If they had ever met the Toad before, they would have known that definitely was not something to say within his hearing.

He immediately quit the job at the mill. He also told my boss I was quitting but if they were ever in the area where we were going to look us up, they were welcome to stay. The first I knew of all of this, I walked in the door after finishing my shift and all my furniture was gone.

My Great-grandmother's rocking chair, my cedar chest and headboard handmade for me by a family friend, an oriental rug that my great-aunt had given me, all gone. Even better, he also sold the shotguns my Dad had asked him to repair for him, antiques and irreplaceable. I threw a fit. All I got back was the bed and cedar chest. He claimed he didn't know the people that bought the rest of the stuff and I was being unreasonable. I noticed he kept his ratty old rocking chair though. We had found it at the dump.

I'm not sure by how much they beat us to Alaska, but we did take the time to drop off our kids at the Toad's parents place near Tillamook, Oregon.

His folks gave us a ride to the Portland airport and we were on our way. The people didn't have a phone, so they got no advance notice to expect us, we were just going. First we landed in Sitka, moved to a smaller plane and then on to Petersburg and finally Wrangell.

The airport is on the other side of the island from town. We were now standing on Wrangell Island, but there was no one here. The terminal was under construction, no one was around. Finally an older car pulled up and the driver stepped out to pick up a parcel that had been left lying on the ground near the unfinished terminal. He looked at us, standing there with our luggage at our feet.

He finally decided we probably weren't ax murderers and asked if someone was meeting us. We said no. He asked if we had a destination in mind? We told him the names of our friends, he thought he knew where they lived so offered us a ride. We accepted.

Town was a few miles from the airstrip. It was all under construction and our flight was one of the first to land on it. That explained the road grader we went around while landing.

He parked on a narrow street above a very tiny frame cabin, perched on pilings on the very steep hillside. We thanked him and dragged out our luggage. We each had a carry on and a large duffle bag. We dragged them down the hill to the shack. This little cabin looked like it probably was a leftover from the Russians and not any of the well to do ones. A power line laying on the ground from a pole near the road looked like an afterthought.

The Toad pushed me in front of him to knock on the door. Oh, so now he wants me to be first in case they didn't really mean it?

Wrangell, Alaska. A rare sunny day.

Chapter 8

The look of shock and surprise would have been priceless if I had not felt so embarrassed by her obvious distress at seeing us.

Her glance down at our luggage only increased the look on her face. They had just received their shipment of food for the winter and every little nook and cranny was filled with cases of food. Even under their bed was stuffed. Their kitchen table folded down from the wall and had a drop down leg to stabilize it. This was probably the tiniest house I have ever seen two adults live in. Now it had four. Her husband and mine were both huge men.

The bathroom was the tiny back porch and there was not room for a tank on the toilet base. You backed onto the seat and pulled the door shut after you and after using you opened the door and flushed by pouring the bucket of water kept outside the door down the toilet, then refilling the bucket at the kitchen sink. Hands were washed at the kitchen sink also which was a single sink with only cold water faucet stuck through the wall over it.

No counter on either side of the sink. Heat was supplied by an oil cookstove. If the table was down, you burned your butt getting by the table and stove. Toad and I slept on the floor under the table and hoped it would not drop on us during the night. The other room of the cabin held a double bed and a dresser stuffed in the walkway near the head of the bed. They crawled on the mattress up to the head of the bed to get in it. We scooted by the foot of the bed to use the bathroom. There were showers available in the bathroom near the docks. Both were unheated bathrooms.

The man worked at the mill located at the end of the road. When he got home that night, she hurried and met him outside before he made it in the door and found us in residence. There were no raised voices, but he was not as pleased to see us as she was and she wasn't. I felt terrible. Neither of these nice people deserved us dumped on them. The Toad was oblivious.

The man got him a job at the mill he worked at and hauled him out with him every morning. The Toad was not all that happy by that turn of events, but did it. The man made no bones about it not being an option.

The lady and I picked berries, canned fish and generally got her supply for winter in fairly good shape and I made the Toad guilty enough he even bought some food at the grocery store.

By the end of the month, Toad got paid and took a leave of absence from work to go back to Oregon. We left and the couple breathed a sigh of relief. They had their house back.

We did not fly home, that was too expensive, we took the ferry to Prince Rupert, then the train from Prince Rupert to Portland, Oregon and a bus to Tillamook. This took about 4 days with no actual sleep.

I had a major migraine headache making me throw up anything I tried eating and lights made my eyes feel like they had pins stabbing into them. My legs had swollen to more than double their usual size.

Toad's parents picked us up at the bus station. While we were gone, they managed to make my sweet son into a rotten little shit. My four and a half year old son reverted to diapers he had not been wearing for more than two years. His mouth opened, he called me a foul name, I smacked him. His grandmother had a heart attack, but since she staged those every time something didn't go her way, I ignored it.

He pee'd the bed that night and I spanked him. She started making excuses. I had enough, finally and stood up for myself and not going to have a whiney 4 year old back in diapers and peeing himself all the time because he was too lazy to move. Now I got to hear what a rotten mother I was for not being nicer to the kids. Hey, they were still alive, weren't they?

Then the grandfather joined in and I finally learned how to win an argument in their house. The one that could yell the loudest, wins. That would be me. I could scream louder than anyone in the entire family. I used to yell across the valley to let the hired man's kids know when we could go out to play and that was over a mile away.

Now we were moving a few thousand miles away from these leeches and I finally learned how to deal with them. Sounds about right for me.

The Toad immediately flew back to Wrangell, leaving me to pack our belongings into the old International pickup we had and drive to Seattle where the ferry terminal was back then.

I stayed at the ranch with my parents and since it was now deer season, I ran the drop-in company with an iron hand. If someone brought in a deer that needed skinned, I charged a quarter of the deer and I picked the quarter. If it needed gutted, that was another quarter and if they had to have bloodshot meat trimmed up or other trim I kept meat accordingly. I cooked for them and cleaned up after them, but they had to bring in firewood every night and it was not used for bonfires. I was not in a good mood and was willing to take it out on all of them. I did not want to move to Alaska.

I knew how to survive here in Oregon and could plant a garden and grow enough to feed the family and get deer for meat. I could even glean from farmers' fields and feed us. None of this was available on that island. I was truly worried that the kids and I would starve in Alaska.

To hunt, a boat was a necessity and I knew we would not be owning a boat. Going by past income, we would be doing good to buy groceries and pay rent. If he quit, there, where would we go and how would we do it? There would be no packing up and just moving.

The 23 times we had moved in the last 6 years didn't instill confidence in me for anything except my ability to pack very well and usually get all the essentials in one load. It was usually the only load.

However, he called and sent the money to pay our passage on the ferry north and said he had a place for us to live already rented. That scared me. He usually picked the scuzziest places imaginable as they were always cheap or he made deals for me to repair them. What was I getting myself and kids into?

I had the guidelines for prices on the ferry. They charged by height as well as by length. So I built a rack for the pickup. All I had to work with were 2x12's and 2x4's. This was a sturdy rack, if nothing else. Six foot five was the cutoff for cheap rates on height so I measured from the ground up to that and stuck a pole here and marked it. Everything had to be under the pole.

We had a 25 cu. Ft. freezer so it went in the load first. The plug in stuck out the back so it could be plugged in any time there was power. I now had parts of eleven deer in that. The friends we had stayed with purchased a beef from my folks. It was cut, wrapped and in there. I placed a layer of blankets and all of our guns went on that and the ammunition for them, beside the freezer.

After that, jars of canned goods Mom and I had done while we harvested the garden during my stay went in. There was not a single box used to pack the truck. Our clothes and blankets worked as cushioning for the canned goods. My cedar chest went on the open tailgate and the headboard. They were both filled completely with canned food. Dishes were stuck in wherever.

As we were getting ready to leave, a friend of the Toads showed up, ready to go. Toad had told him he could come with me. Yeah, as jealous as the Toad was, I didn't believe it and until Toad told me on the phone I still didn't.

We left the next morning, leaving his jealous wife behind and headed to my jealous husband. We should have just moved right on into Canada and left them both. I'm sure we could have each found better partners somewhere else. The rear axle broke on the freeway in Portland, Oregon. We could see a repair shop on the other side of the overpass we were stopped near. All the streets went the wrong way and we would have had to either walk back to the last exit or ahead to the next exit to get over there. The guy with me walked over and talked the shop owner into coming to get us.

He could see us from his door. He drove over with his pretty new tow truck and brand new equipment. He jacked up the back, the jack wilted under the weight of the truck, he backed up the tow truck and lifted the back and set the four wheeled dolly under, let the truck down and all four tires went flat on the dolly. He started yelling at me about what did I have in that truck, anyway, lead?

By this time, he was in a very bad mood. He winched the back of the truck up again and told the guy with me to hold the steering wheel straight and he took us up the down ramp of the freeway and across the overpass going the wrong direction until he reached his shop. Cars were honking at us and barely missing us as they whizzed by.

He got inside the shop and told us if we said that just happened, he would deny it. The entire tow was illegal. He took his time, but he did repair the axle. My final paycheck just covered it. However, we reached the dock in time to see the ferry we were supposed to be on, going over the horizon. Now what to do? We had just enough money to reach Wrangell. But if we went back to the ranch to wait until the next ferry, next week, we would not have enough money to pay for the ferry. How hard could it be to drive on up through Canada and catch the ferry at Prince Rupert? We turned north.

We were tired, but kept driving. Taking turns and trying to talk enough to keep each other awake. Then a State policeman stopped us, thinking we were drunk. After talking to us, he told us to pull over at the next motel and sleep. He followed us to make sure we did.

We got up the next morning to possible food poisoning but we headed north again, anyway. We didn't pass a single rest area and few service stations without stopping though and all of us were totally miserable.

We pulled up at some little out of the way Border Crossing as we also didn't have a map, just turned on any road that said north. We arrived as they were almost ready to change shifts. The new guard would not start until the current guard was through with us.

The only thing he asked for that I had handy was the registration papers for the pickup. No insurance card, no cash minimum, no vet's certificate for the cat hiding under the seat. The kids were looking longingly at the rest room just on the other side of the Border, begging to go potty. My teeth were missing as I had not been able to get my teeth finished before we moved. Then he asked about guns. Why yes, we have a lot of them.

He decided he needed to look under that nailed down oiled canvas tarp I had nailed securely over the load. I did have a hammer handy and handed it to him as he started looking for a way to look under the tarp. The 16 penny nails did their job well. He finally got a couple of the nails pried loose and raised the corner of the tarp and shined his flashlight under it. "OHMYGOD."

He hurriedly nailed the tarp back down, handed back the hammer and told us to just go. The other guard was doubled over laughing. We assumed north, so drove over to the rest room the kids needed badly by this time and so did I. We spent quite a while in there and then resumed our trek north.

Wrangell harbor, Alaska, by Claire McGill

Chapter 9

We had a flat tire on the front left tire a short ways up the road. We pulled over and were sitting there trying to remember where the jack got put when a friendly fellow stopped and offered to help. He and my passenger quickly got it changed and back on the road again. The problem soon showed up. He had placed the jack under the tie rod. Now 35 mph was our top speed without going off the road.

One of my Mom's childhood friends lived just south of Quesnel, BC. They had remained pen pals since second grade. I had met her years before and knew we should stop and visit a little while. Her husband helped remove the bent tie rod. They placed it bent side up and set a jack on the bend and jacked up the pickup again. That straightened that tie rod right out. Back on the road yet again.

We got to Prince Rupert that evening just in time to see the ferry we were supposed to be on chug right on by. That one didn't stop at Prince Rupert. The one the next day was aground on a small island somewhere. The one the day after was in dry dock. I livened up our stay in Prince Rupert by having another miscarriage. Yeah, I was having such a fun trip.

    Finally we were loaded on a ferry heading to Wrangell. The kids and I were on first name basis with all the neat little shops in Prince Rupert and the owners fed them enough free samples that they seldom needed real meals. We always had breakfast at the Chinese place that had dozens of men working behind the counter and the menu numbered on a board above the counter. It was safest to point at the one you wanted.

    We found a wonderful cheese and sausage shop and bought as much as we could afford. It was surprisingly inexpensive and the kids ate more than we bought, I think.

    The ferry ride north was nice and the kids loved it. They made friends all over the boat. The crew took them to meet the captain up on the bridge. He let them steer the boat. They were the only children on the entire ship so got royal treatment and they were back to being well behaved, so that helped, also. A month at my parents place and me home too, had taught them their manners again.

    We docked in Wrangell late in the afternoon and it was just getting dusk. Over the sounds of the ship and motors of vehicles starting to drive off, the loud tones of the Toad bellowing "where the hell you been and who you been messing around with", echoed over the deck. Ah yes, together again.

Home was a 2 bedroom trailer house in an extremely crowded trailer park halfway out the road toward the mill the Toad worked at.

With no place else to go, my passenger moved in with us. Then somehow the friend of my brother that used to stay with us a lot in Oregon showed up, then my ex-boss from the café. This all jammed into the 2 bedroom trailer was a bit crowded so then wives started showing up, too. Everyone immediately got jobs at the mills, so work was not a problem although both mills are shut down now. But it took a month to receive the first check so each person had to stay at least a month before affording to move out.

My passenger coming up was the first one to move out. He had been friends with the Toad, but after being around him nonstop, they no longer were friends. Then my ex-boss moved into the trailer beside us. Brothers' friend Sonny stayed and stayed and stayed. He managed to get married just before he left to come up to Alaska so now his wife wanted to join him, said she was pregnant. She had a small daughter.

I was not enthusiastic about them all living with us. We told her if she came, to only bring necessities as there just wasn't room and her family could ship up her stuff later when they found themselves a place to live. She said she understood perfectly. I explained we were eating what we harvested from the ocean and whatever we could barter, she said she had no problem with that, would eat anything. It was going to be an adventure. She had already booked her ticket and was arriving the next morning.

There was a large minus tide that morning, so I had gone clam digging beyond the end of the road. I found a huge bed of geoducs and filled a trashcan we used only for seafood full of huge ones. I was sitting on the floor under the table cleaning them as that was the only place there was room when I heard her voice the first time. It gave the same reaction as fingernails on chalkboard. Nasal, whiney with no inflection whatsoever whether she was happy, sad or furious.

Then she stepped through the door and I swear the trailer tilted. Then her whine changed from complaining about the rain to complaining about the odor of the clams I was cleaning. Her husband finished boosting her up the step into the house and stepped in after her. He was carrying the cutest little delicate baby I have ever seen. I thought she was 7 or 8 months old, dressed in frills and white socks and black shoes.

The Toad and a friend were lugging two huge suitcases in as soon as they cleared the doorway. One was full of prescription medications, the other was full of diapers and bottles, no clothes whatsoever for either one of them.

The woman waddled over to the couch and plopped into it and only moved to go to the bathroom. The child was sat on the couch beside her and stayed right where she was put. I made clam chowder and homemade bread for dinner that evening. I started to give the baby a bite of the chowder and got the whole, no, she can't eat that, she is allergic to everything but milk spiel.

Then the mother went through her suitcase of pills and took one of each every single day. She didn't even know what most were for and I only hoped most were placebos. She didn't like homemade bread, wouldn't eat clam chowder, either.

Soon all the bottles were dirty and the mother had yet to rouse herself off the couch to wash them. I was starting to get the drift of how this was going to work out.

I started giving the baby a spoonful of broth and wait a day to see if there was a reaction, then add something else. I found out the baby was just over 2 years old.

The mother only spoke baby talk to her so of course she didn't speak. I didn't understand baby talk so she had to speak correctly for me and learned very fast and was housebroke in one day. After all, all the diapers were now dirty and left where the mother dropped them. All the dirty bottles were lined up on the kitchen sink.

When her mother tried putting a diaper on her she got indignant and told her those were just for babies. Her mother about fainted. Not only was her kid out of diapers, she could walk, eat real food and talk. Even worse, she started growing. I guess the mother liked having a perpetual baby.

The family with 12 kids from Prairie City that helped me repair one of the houses moved up here when we did, but rented a huge house in town instead of moving in with us. I didn't even know they had arrived. Now they were getting ready to move back to Oregon, she didn't like it here. They came and let us know they were moving so we could go see about renting their house. I loved that house and we soon made a deal with the landlord to rent it just as it sat. The owner wouldn't even have to clean it first.

Houses to rent on an island are few and far between and even the trailers are usually all occupied. We moved and instead of Sonny and his irritating wife and sweet little girl staying and renting this trailer, they moved in with us. Dang, can't even move away from them.

We thoroughly cleaned and even did some repairs underneath the house. It was built on a steep side hill as all of the town is, pretty much. Instead of digging out a level spot to build, they had built touching the hill on the uphill section and on a 2x4 wall framing in the front and tapering up to the hill in back. These were not milled 2x4's, they were odd sizes and the house was built before electricity was expected to be on the island.

The ceilings were 14 foot in the entire house, except where they were higher in the large open room between upstairs bedrooms. It may have been a ballroom as the house had a parlor, sitting room and library. There was a butler's pantry and maid's quarters. Stored under the eaves were ancient curved top mariners trunks, brass bound. I would have loved to have most of the furniture and the trunks or just to have stayed in the house, I loved it.

The dining room had built in china closets along one entire wall with leaded glass doors and old mirrors under the upper cabinets. The table had 13 leaves to add and after it was pulled out so far, legs dropped down to stabilize it. The other wall to the outdoors had floor to ceiling windows.

There was an old fashioned chair in the sitting room. The back reclined and it had metal rods to place in metal spacers to hold the back in position. The arms were carved lions heads and the legs were carved lions feet. It was a very comfortable chair and very large. Both kids could sit in it with me to be read to.

The kitchen was a huge bare room. A table on one side and an oil drip cookstove on the other that worked as the source of heat for the house, heated the hot water and to cook on. The hot water had to be left dripping at one of the faucets or the tank tended to explode. Then there was the butler's pantry as a nice room off to one side of the kitchen. It was floor to ceiling cabinets, cupboards, bins and counter space with countertop to ceiling windows on the exterior wall. I used the maids' room as a pantry for canned goods.

The bathroom had a huge claw footed tub in the center. My kids and half the neighborhood kids used it as an indoor pool. I supplied body crayons and they painted themselves, each other and the tub. Swimsuits were required. They couldn't actually swim in it if anyone else was in it with them, but they could get a couple of strokes back and forth. Very short laps.

The room we used as our bedroom had another very large room attached that was large enough for another bedroom, except it opened into our room and had no windows. I used it as a closet.

Finally I lived in a house with enough storage room that I was a good housekeeper. Joe, the only male on the island allowed to continue to wear his hair long although everyone called him Sue, moved in with us. He was just discharged from the Navy. He lied about his age and they didn't find out until a bit before his actual discharge was due, when he asked about re-upping and they found out how old he really was. He would have had his legal-to-join birthday just before he would sign to re-up. That boy was a wonder at mopping floors and loved to do it. He could mop that entire house in short order. He said it was simple compared to a battle ship. He volunteered to mop and did it once a week. Top to bottom, that house was clean.

He also was a bottomless pit when it came to eating. He told me I could not afford to feed him for the price I charged for his room, so he would sign over his checks and ask for $25 back as spending money during the week for snacks. He worked at the mill with the Toad and Sonny. I baked a cake every day and made bread every other day. I usually had a large pot of stew or chowder going no matter what dinner was going to be as everyone ate whenever besides meals.

The fat cow stayed in bed until she got hungry, then would come cook herself breakfast. She would fry a full pan of potatoes, almost a dozen eggs and if there was bacon she could find, a pound of bacon. She did not share this with the kids, including her own. She would sit right there at the table, with both arms around her dish like she thought one of the kids was going to take something off her plate and the kids would be standing around the table salivating. I finally told her if she was cooking, to at least share with the kids.

She never got dressed until she expected the men to get home from work. Usually she stayed in bed until about a half hour before they were due home, then get dressed and when she saw them park down at the foot of the stairs coming up to the house, she would grab something and immediately act so overworked. I was a slave driver and the whole bit. I really wanted to hurt her. The house had three large rooms across the front and they used the one I considered a library as their bedroom. It would have been a beautiful library, floor to ceiling shelves and lovely windows.

A friend of ours owned a shrimp boat and we would go help pull nets once in a while, then he would fill our seafood trash can with shrimp for our help. He had a standing invitation to dinner and always showed up with a 5 gallon bucket of shrimp.

One afternoon he came to visit and she had not bothered to get dressed yet. Her bathrobe had two buttons. One about her navel and one about her neck. She stood in the arched doorway between the dining room and living room and posed prettily, one arm over her head against the door frame and the other on her ample hip. The poor man turned beet red, sputtered and left. He always made sure she was fully dressed after that when he came by and his visits were much farther between.

She had been going on about being pregnant for months, finally she actually was. The woman seldom moved and had absolutely no muscle tone. If she made it down the steps, the kids all got behind her and pushed her to help her make it back up the steps. In the house if she was mad at the kids, they ran upstairs, they knew she couldn't make it up there without help.

I spaded up a garden and planted it uphill from the house. It helped keep me from strangling her. During this time, I had yet another miscarriage. Finally a doctor came to visit the island that would do a vasectomy on the Toad as birth control seemed to never work for me. I got pregnant using everything available at that time.

I liked Wrangell. The people, the attitude, everything and I could handle the weather. Even though it rained a lot, it also had a lot of sunshine and everything dried out in about a half hour after the rain stopped. Coming in the boat harbor from sea, there was a sign on a piling right out in the middle. "Welcome to Wrangell, Home of 2000 Happy Souls and 500 Soreheads." I always liked that sign.

Wrangell, Alaska. I really loved it there, once we got there. I really hated leaving it.

Chapter 10

I reloaded ammunition for the men all week, then we would go shooting targets on the weekends. The men had plastic bullets powered by the primers that they used as target loads in the house, firing at a target pinned to a sheet hung in an open doorway.

Sonny, practicing quick draw shot himself in the back of the leg and knocked himself down. Then he play-slapped the Toad across the face, challenging him to a duel and the Toad told him to quit, he did it again and the Toad pulled his gun and chased Sonny out the door. Sonny ran the length of the porch as the Toad swung out the door then shot him in the shoulder with the plastic bullet. It had more power than expected and Sonny went right on over the railing into the large shrub under the railing.

It was a sunny day so everyone in town was outside enjoying the weather and had heard all the shooting in the house and saw the shooting on the porch. There were no police there at that time and no one knew what to do. Sonny finally untangled from the shrub and walked out by the road, then climbed the stairs, rubbing his shoulder and town breathed a sigh of relief.

We were finally getting some hot weather and everyone thought they were going to have to barge water to the town from the mainland.

The fat one decided she was not only going to go watch the shooting, she was going to shoot. This was the person that wouldn't walk anywhere and now she was going to hike to the target area and shoot, out in the hottest weather we had all summer.

She grabbed one of the 44 magnums and stood behind the bench, as she had seen the men do. Her husband stood up to go assist her and she snarled at him. She had grabbed a beer from the cooler and chugged it down as she stood there, waiting her turn. Then she grabbed another. She screamed at him that she was an adult and she knew what she was doing. Okay.

She stuck the gun out in front of her and held it like a stick, pulled the trigger and smacked herself in the forehead with the barrel, plopped on the ground and sat there, dazed. Yup, she knew how to do that perfectly. Never saw it done better in my life.

I know I am not being kind to her, but that woman grated on my nerves so bad I would start shaking whenever I heard her voice.

We stopped at a friend's house on the way home that wanted to blow up a tree stump in his yard. He had the dynamite, caps and fuse, he wasn't sure about placing the powder though. Yeah, like we knew anything other than our fishing experience, but I did remember my Dad saying it had to be drilled in and then covered or it just blew back out the hole.

The guys started drilling some large holes to shove the sticks down into the base. I went inside with the man's wife, the fat one sat on the stump and drank more beer. She was very fair and having spent no time outdoors all summer, she was more than white, she was fish belly white.

By the end of this day she was totally sunburned as she was also prone to pulling her shirt down over her shoulders and trying to look sexy. Her skirt was hiked up her legs and her blouse was pulled down, so when she got sunburned, she really got sunburned.

They finally got her to move so they could light the fuses. She just got in the trailer house when the yard exploded. It felt like the trailer rocked up on its side. The hole in the ground was impressive. The entire stump was sitting across the highway from the house.

She wasn't feeling great by the time we got home. She went into the bathroom and sneezed while on the toilet and gave partial birth to a poor little malformed boy.

I got her into her bed and called the hospital as this week they had a doctor visiting. The man would not come over to the house, it was about 4 blocks away. I didn't have a car at home and could not get her back down those stairs. There was no ambulance. Then he hung up on me. I checked her and she still only had half the baby hanging out. Then she pushed him the rest of the way out. He was so small, not even the weight of a pound of butter. The tiniest human. He never had a chance at life.

I wrapped him and placed him over on the dresser. She started bleeding heavily. I remembered what they did to me when I had my daughter and started kneading her belly, trying to get it to tighten up.

She was like kneading soft bread dough. My arms sank into her huge belly and I could not find any muscle in there anywhere. I finally found the uterus and kneaded it to stop the bleeding.

The men finally got home and we made a litter of sorts from a heavy quilt and the men carried her down those 46 steps to the pickup and hauled her to the hospital.

The doctor bawled everyone out and was a general ass. He inspected the baby, said it was better off and left the room. I didn't like the woman, but I was at least fairly civil to her and now I figured I probably even saved her sorry hide.

She managed to stay in the hospital over a week, saying she would have to work if she came home.

They felt so sorry for poor overworked her. Then I was back to wanting to hit her.

She and Sonny had been having some problems as he wasn't totally blind and saw how much work she did and how she left the care and raising of her daughter to me. The little girl had grown over a foot in just a few months, getting real food. She now looked the age she was and was a happy hyper little girl that fit right in with my two. The fat one took her daughter and went home to Idaho.

The Toad started pushing me whenever he wanted to make sure I was going to do what he wanted. One evening he came in the door from work and we had just finished waxing all the floors. I was wearing a pair of old socks as no one wore shoes in the house there. He used both hands, fingers stiff to jab my shoulders, knocking me back. He didn't stop, he just kept walking and jabbing me as I scrambled to stay on my feet. I stayed upright all through the living room, dining room and almost made the kitchen when my feet lost the race with gravity. The back of my head was the first thing to land and it was on the sharp corner of the kitchen door sill. It sounded like dropping a ripe watermelon. He just dumped me on the couch and I went right to sleep. After several hours, I finally woke up to the kids wanting dinner. My balance was messed up. I still have a small dent.

The Toad quit his job right after my Mom came to visit and we rode back to Prince Rupert on the ferry with her. The Toad struck up a conversation with a fellow that lived near Fairbanks. Another person learned the hard way not to casually invite someone to stop by.

Toad sold our old pickup to the boy living with us, Sue, and bought an even older crewcab pickup, sight unseen from a dealer in Ketchikan. Of course a used car dealer would never lie about the condition of a vehicle now would he?

The pickup was finally delivered the day before we were supposed to leave on the ferry. Almost a week late. The Toad had also bought a small trailer as it looked like that pickup might not make it and Sue offered to drive up with us and haul a load and tow the trailer. The new-to-us pickup was rust colored, then I found some white paint on it and the paperwork said white.

We carried the packed boxes down those stairs and had that truck loaded to the limit within plenty of time and the ladies from our Church came over and helped clean the entire house with Sue running the mop bucket. That house was spotless. The landlord came over to inspect and said it was a sty and we would not get our deposit back. We needed that money. He was adamant and left. I wanted to cry. Instead I got vindictive.

I took the open bag of flour from the flour bin and whirled my way through the rooms. The open can of shortening went over all the windows. Then we drove down and loaded on the ferry headed north. Not an adult moment. I still feel a little guilty about that.

The Alaska Range, south of Fairbanks, Alaska.
Photo by Liz Smarr

Chapter 11

    The trip north started damp and chilly. It was the first week of October, 1970 and we were moving to Fairbanks, Alaska. I knew nothing about Fairbanks. I had heard rumors and none of them were good. The windshield wipers didn't work on the truck and we hit snow before the Canadian Border. Then Sue went off the road, and we had to stop and try getting him back on the highway.

    While we were stopped, I found some fish line under the seat and tied it from one wiper arm, around through the wing window, out the other wing window, to the other wiper arm and finally to the first wiper again. Then I was the wiper motor for several hundred miles of snow and blizzard conditions as we kept going north. The trailer of our household goods was left behind. Broken spring on the trailer. All my taxidermy supplies were on it, including the 60 gallon wooden barrels used for tanning hides. Plus a lot of our food. I knew it, we were going to starve.

    There was several inches of snow on the ground when we arrived. Toad called the man he had talked to on the ferry. Another shocked silence, followed by hesitant directions on how to reach their home. They lived in a two bedroom trailer house off Badger Road between North Pole and Fairbanks. The wife was definitely not happy to see all of us descending on her. Their little boy was probably the only one that was happy.

    She sent her husband to town for fried chicken for dinner and all the side dishes. Then we placed sleeping bags wall to wall practically, in their living room for sleeping as he had to be at work early the next morning. She arranged a place for us to rent at 6 mile Village trailer park. I doubt if Toad contributed to the rent.

    Toad found work immediately at the tire shop on South Cushman. Sue and Sonny unpacked everything that managed to make the entire trip, into the little trailer with wannigan that was now our home.

    It had started out as a travel trailer with fold down bunks in the hallway going back to the bedroom in the back. The bathroom was all metal with a fold out sink and a fold up toilet and the entire room became the shower. The kitchen/dining area took up the rest of the trailer and it had a propane cook stove that scared me to death. Someone else always had to light it for me to cook.

    The added wannigan was two larger rooms, one was used as a living room and the other as our bedroom. Everything was stored in our bedroom so there was room to walk in the other rooms. Sue and Sonny took the back bedroom in the trailer and the kids got the fold down bunks.

About a week after we moved in, I was just getting up to get the kids ready for school when it sounded like a semi-truck rumbling in the distance but getting closer and closer, then WHAM. It hit the house. I almost fell against the bed and was getting really mad. That idiot neighbor truck driver was drunk again. About then, the radio announcer said "WOW, did you feel that one! A real banger." It was my first earthquake.

Our friend from Wrangell that used to shrimp had sold his boat and moved up here late in the summer. He found us and moved in, also. He had been working for a fellow on Chena Hot Springs Road, building custom cabinets in the man's house in exchange for a parcel of land on the homestead the man was subdividing.

The man let him have the lot against the back property line and no access was in, so Frank paid for all the road building to his lot besides building beautiful cabinets and all the finish work in the fancy large log home above the road. The work was finished now and the man told Frank he had to move off the lot as it was sold, now. None of the deal was on paper, it was a handshake deal and Frank was the loser on it. The man got wonderfully finished interior on his home and a road built to specs on his subdivision. Frank got zilch.

Sue didn't like the snow and cold so he packed up the old International pickup from Oregon and went back to Wrangell. Frank decided to see what it was like down on the Kenai. The oil pipeline was on hold and everyone was leaving Fairbanks in droves. We had not been here quite a month when the Toad stormed in and said he had quit his job.

Two kids were renting a tiny travel trailer just behind ours that didn't have heat or water in it. They were married, she was pregnant and no one would hire them as they looked about 12 and 13. They were actually 18 and 19 but no one believed them. They were freezing to death and down to the bag of oatmeal. That certainly brought back memories to me. We started asking them to help us eat our meals as I still had not learned to cut down quantities now that Sue was gone. Then we found out about the no heat, either. So they moved in with us.

We rented a larger trailer out on Dennis Road just before the Toad quit. It had gone through the huge flood in 1967 and all the insulation from halfway up the walls had dropped. It had two bedrooms. They were very small, but there were two of them. It had a regular propane cook stove and a double oven set built into one wall. Three ovens with pilot lights. I loved that part of it.

Five adults, two small children and three cats living in a very confined area is not a great way to spend an extremely cold snowy winter. I shoveled a lot of snow. I shoveled it up against the trailer and far to the sides. A truck could have driven around this trailer.

By this time, our pickup was not running. The weather had deteriorated to extremely cold and snowing. I am still waiting to see it get too cold to snow. Sonny had decided to thin the oil with gasoline to help the truck start easier. That took out the motor as the oil now had no lubricating ability from all the gas. He had drained most of the oil and refilled the entire oil reservoir with gas. Yes, the truck started, it was 40 below zero and didn't have plug in heaters, but he wanted to go to town, so he got it started and they went. They didn't shut it off in town as it was running really rough but when they shut it off at the trailer, it seized up and never moved again on its own power.

Now we were stranded about 8 miles from town, which doesn't sound like much, but none of us had winter gear for this climate. Most of our canned food was sitting on the trailer back near Haines. We had no money coming in since Toad quit his job and was ineligible for unemployment. I had used even the change out of the piggy banks buying food.

At that time, in Alaska, you had to buy food stamps. Yes, you got more value in food than what you paid for the coupons, but if you were flat broke, you could not get food stamps. The neighbor lady told me about food stamps but didn't mention that part.

The neighbor worked in town and let me catch a ride in with her. She dropped me off at the right building downtown. She would pick me up there, that evening for the ride home. The State office for Assistance was located upstairs in a building by the theatre on 2nd Avenue. The line, even this early in the morning was clear out of the office down the hall and starting down the stairs.

At least it was warm inside the building. I only had a regular jacket and was wearing a vest under it, a sweater and a T shirt, regular jeans, a pair of socks and moccasins. Really something to be out in minus 40 and 50 degree weather in.

The State had a standing offer at that time, a ticket home after signing a paper that you would never return. I really wanted to go home to my parents, but Daddy's warning that I would not be welcome still rang through my mind. He had renewed it before I left to drive to Seattle.

The State did pay our rent and utility bill up so we didn't get evicted. Then she told me I would be eligible for food stamps in an amount that made me happy inside, I could buy groceries for the kids. Then she told me that would be $25 for the coupon books. What? If I had $25 I would not be here begging, I would have bought food.

She sent me out in the hall while they took a break and locked up the office after kicking everyone out, for lunch. Others in line must have been used to this as people were pulling sandwiches out of pockets and sodas. I sat on the floor and tears slid down my cheeks. I would not give in and actually cry, but once in a while, a tear still made its way out.

I knew it, move up here where I couldn't just go kill a deer and my kids were going to starve. If there was anything edible growing here, it certainly wasn't out where I could find it. The snow continued to fall and the temperatures continued to drop.

When the lunch break was over, the woman called me back in and they did give me some food stamps. Not the amount she had told me to start with, but she asked if that would give me groceries for a week and come back in next week and she would see what she could do. I have always felt that woman may have paid for the food stamps for me on her own. She probably saved us.

I had several hours before getting picked up for the ride home, so walked to the closest grocery store and spent the coupons on dry beans and rice. Not exactly tasty fare, but we would not starve. A box of bacon ends was really cheap, so I got one to add flavor to the assorted types of beans in the bag. A box of dried milk rounded out my shopping. The kids would have rice with sugar and milk for breakfast before going to school. I still had some sugar and cinnamon at the trailer. It would fill them up, even though they would probably hate it for life, once they didn't have to eat it to have food.

I walked back to the office building with my purchases and was happy to get back inside. I was freezing. I couldn't feel my feet and I didn't feel good. I had been feeling ill for quite a while.

One of the office workers asked if I was okay and made an appointment for me to see a doctor next week, the same day I was supposed to be back in here. We all got free medical.

I rode home and unloaded the groceries. Toad helped unpack the bags and immediately got upset that I had not bought his soda. He had to have his soda no matter whether we had food or not. Bad me, I only bought actual food for the rest of us.

When I went back in, somehow the lady had managed to get unemployment started for the Toad. I still don't know how she managed that. Now we had some actual cash coming in and I started keeping the change back so it didn't get spent. Toad knew I had to have so much each month to buy the food stamp coupons, so he only gave me that much, but since it was demeaning for him to use food stamps, he would send enough cash in with me to buy his soda, as I refused to buy it on the food stamps and told him stores wouldn't accept food stamps for soda pop.

My blood tests showed something not right with my blood and they did more tests. So each month when I went in to shop, I also got more blood tests.

Toad continued to act like a jealous ass and accused me of sleeping with Sonny and the young man still living with us. Even though he was right there, all the time, he still accused. When was I supposed to be doing all this? He never needed things to make sense. I thought maybe if I got really fat, he would give it up. Didn't work and I have had trouble keeping weight off ever since. A really stupid idea.

Evenings, we sat around and ate chips and dip and played card games. Mainly solitaire for me while the guys played poker or cribbage. The pregnant girl joined their game or watched. I got really fat. Even with all the shoveling, I ballooned. I gained until I was well over 200 pounds.

As winter progressed, the neighbor started having her husband drive her back and forth as the weather was even colder. He was going in around noon and would pick us both up that evening.

I sat at the clinic, waiting until they closed and locked the doors. Then I walked to Foodland and waited there, as they usually stopped there to shop before going home. I stayed there until the doors closed and locked. Now I was locked out of the only places I knew, it was 56 degrees below zero F. and I was dressed as usual as that was all I had to wear. I did have a piece of cardboard cut as insoles in my moccasins.

I found a payphone on the corner of Gaffney and Cushman Streets but it was too cold to work. A few cabs went by but none would stop. I kept walking.

26th Street Market was still open and I stumbled inside, too cold to talk. I finally could ask if I could warm up. The owner let me. A cab pulled up and the driver came in to buy a bottle of liquor to deliver somewhere. I asked if he was still driving and he said he still had a couple of hours before his shift ended. I asked if he would give me a ride home. He said yes, so when he left, I went with him and got in the cab. He told me he would come back for me but I didn't want to take chances and the store was getting ready to close.

I rode along on his delivery, then he flipped the meter and started it running again for my trip home. I didn't tell him until we pulled up that I had to go in for the money to pay him. I stumbled into the trailer, my feet were in agony by now and told the Toad to go pay the cab. He bitched about the expense, but he did it.

I went in the bathroom and ran the tub full of warm water, stripped down and got in. I sat there crying as I thawed out. The bottoms of my feet made huge water blisters hanging down as they thawed. My toes were hard to find under the huge blisters. When I finally got out of the tub, I dried off carefully, pulled on my sleep wear and crawled to bed, I could not walk. The neighbor's excuse? Ha-ha, he forgot me and took his wife out to dinner.

Since I now refused to hitch hike in for groceries anymore and my feet were not in any condition to even try, it was now up to the rest of the household to figure out buying groceries.

Sonny found a job as baker at one of the stores in town and got a room. The young couple got a check from his Dad and they moved into town. Toad took one of our kittens outside and shot it in a barrel. What a big man.

I got fat but he got hugely obese over the winter. He found a house to rent in the town of North Pole. North Pole didn't have any place to shop, but it had a post office and he no longer allowed me to get mail delivered to the house.

I also could not get the mail from our mailbox in front of the trailer, by the time we left there. One day I walked up to get it, he backed the pickup he had just bought up the driveway after me. I jumped and grabbed the tailgate, he kept backing and dragging me backwards up onto the main road. I was screaming and banging on the truck with one fist the whole way, but he didn't stop until a neighbor ran out and stopped him. My ribs were badly bruised from impact with the tailgate and my poor feet were scraped raw from dragging on the gravel. I still think he was trying for a cheap divorce, right there. He claimed he didn't know I was there and didn't hear me. The neighbors a couple of acres away could, though.

He would do things like this, then say "I love you." I certainly didn't feel like saying that back to him. He usually said it while hugging me so hard it hurt, in front of people so if I struggled to get loose, it looked like I was being a bitch.

This day, he pulled that after the neighbor got him stopped from dragging me. I stayed quiet. He "playfully" grabbed harder and said, "come on, you know you love me too." I still didn't say anything. Then he swung me around so hard my neck snapped and said, "I said I love you, don't you love me?"

Well, no, I don't. Besides, if this was him loving me, I doubt if I could survive too much more of it. We walked back into the trailer and he slammed the door behind us. Then he demanded I tell him I loved him. "No, I don't and right this minute, I don't much like you, either."

I guess he expected me to lie or something, but he certainly looked surprised.

That winter saw a total official snowfall of 145 inches which was the record at that time and an unofficial record cold of minus 80 degrees although the official cold wasn't that much. Out where we lived in the low swamps, it was very cold.

Chapter 12

Life was a little tense around there while we moved to the new house. The well had been frozen up for the last few weeks and the landlord wanted us out so he could repair it. This was the first place we moved out of with the landlord still liking us and we didn't owe back rent. Thanks to the State.

The dumpy little house we moved into backed onto a tiny little deep lake. I was worried about the kids falling over the steep bank into it, but the Toad wasn't worried at all. He started work at the railroad.

We now lived close enough to school for my daughter to walk to school and walked part of the way with three kids she went to school with. Two were in my daughter's class and the third one would be in my son's class next year. They had a very little brother at home. My son would have been in kindergarten, but it was half days and we just now lived close enough to walk as until now, we didn't have a vehicle to take him. Buses didn't run for kindergarten.

The parents, Willy and Sue, came over and got acquainted. Then they stayed for dinner. Then they all started spending the night. They were living in a one room building behind the bar across the main highway and railroad tracks from our place.

Then her parents, Ralph and Mabel, stopped by and started staying for dinner.

An ad in the newspaper caught my eye and I was excited to know we might be able to afford some land. Land had been super cheap all winter, but it was in large parcels and we could not pay for it, even when it dropped to $15 an acre. This ad was for 10 acre parcels down near Delta at $29.50 a month. $29.50 down.

We drove down and liked the area, so made the deal for 10 acres. Then we drove down almost every weekend to start clearing an area to build. Too bad there wasn't any work in the area.

This landlord lived next door to us. The wife was an alcoholic but a fairly nice one. The day our rent was due, she was at the door bright and early, asking for it but forgot her receipt book. Toad handed over the cash. Her husband got home from work and she was out so he came over and asked for the rent. We told him we gave it to his wife and he got upset. He should have told us to never give her money if he didn't want her having it. The next day he told us to find another place, he didn't believe we paid the rent.

Toad still had the job working on the railroad. The section house was only a couple of blocks from our house, yet he still took the pickup to work because I might use it.

Twice a month, I got to go to Fairbanks shopping. Usually Sue, her 4 kids, me and my 2 kids all went in together in that small pickup. Toad questioned each and every one of them about who we saw, talked to or might have seen while we were in town. All of our stories better match.

Somehow Toad heard about a house for rent, even cheaper than the dump we just got told to leave. This house was a one bedroom house built similar to a trailer house design, only insulated with sawdust. It was fairly old and located on a road inhabited only by a group of people believing in a single religion. We would be the only heathens living on the entire road. Of course he took the house.

Then we found that the well didn't work, the sewer lines were blocked and the back half of the house was totally unusable due to extreme leaking. We moved in anyway. The area we could use was the front room which was a combo kitchen/living room, 15 x 15 feet, and the small hallway which would hold the set of used military surplus bunk beds we found for the kids.

We would sleep on the living room floor. If we were careful where we set things in the bedroom, we could store boxes of our belongings back there and covered them with a tarp.

We hauled water from the railroad section house, used the railroad showers and for a toilet, we used a bucket.

We moved in early enough in the summer to plant a garden, so I did get one spaded up and planted. We were shunned by the neighbors and they were convinced Toad was Satan. Hmmm, maybe they had something there.

The kids started playing with a dog that hung around the house all the time so soon considered it their dog and named it Dodo Bird. It was a nice dog, well behaved and friendly.

Toad made friends with the son of one of the women that lived farther down the road. The man was in his late 20's but had polio as a child. Somehow, because he had been so ill and his body didn't always function as well as it should, his family acted and treated him as though his mind was affected also. He never went back to school. No one taught him manners, he didn't know how to read. We had another child in our group that happened to be as old as we were.

Ray managed to be there for dinner every evening but he did bring food for me to cook. I started teaching him some table manners. He got a check every month and did use it fairly wisely. He also was a good mechanic, teaching himself. He kept an old pickup in excellent shape and worked on our piece of junk quite often.

Halloween was not observed in any way by our neighbors, however for the week after Halloween, all their kids stopped by in their way home from school to get candy.

A few days before Thanksgiving, Ray asked what all I needed to make a real Thanksgiving dinner. I told him my oven didn't work and I wasn't sure exactly how I was going to make dinner.

He was surprised and then said he wondered why nothing was ever cooked in the oven, only on top the stove. The stove had 4 burners, but one didn't work at all, one worked on high only, one worked on medium and the other worked on low. So I had to get things going on one, move that pot to the next burner and so on, until I had dinner ready. I did make cookies on the griddle I had.

The next day, Ray backed his pickup up to our door and unloaded a nice used propane cookstove, with a tank and regulator. He installed the whole thing and hauled off the pathetic electric stove that we had. Then he brought in everything needed for a really sumptuous Thanksgiving dinner. He said he asked a lady at the store what was needed. I started making pies. Ray was my taste tester.

He and the kids all sampled enough that the first night I didn't have to cook dinner for them, they were all so full of pie. Willy and Sue showed up almost every day for dinner also, so we had quite a group there for dinner.

Ralph and Mabel came over for Thanksgiving, also. Ray had never had a Thanksgiving dinner and the rest of the folks along that road were all upset at him for socializing with us and eating at our house. He didn't care.

I had taught the Toad to read for pleasure over the years and now taught Ray to read, also. He learned quickly and was seldom without a book in a pocket or his truck. The man was not dumb, he was just untaught.

The day after Thanksgiving, the entire neighborhood smelled like turkey roasting and they rationalized by saying turkey was so cheap. They did the same thing at Christmas. They bought stuff for their kids, but didn't wrap anything or decorate, and did it the day after Christmas.

They would leave their small children locked in the houses during the day while they went around, knocking on doors and making nuisances of themselves doing penance. It is not that they expect to convert anyone. Walking down the road, the sound of kids crying or fighting or whatever in the houses could be heard from the road.

One of the neighbors shot Dodo Bird and the kids were heartbroken.

Ray's brother, Earl, worked part time for a tire shop in Fairbanks. Not the one Toad worked in when we first got here. He was also just about to get out of the military. The mascot for Fort Wainwright was a husky dog. The dog didn't like the sound made by small yappy dogs and the new Base Commander raised little poodles.

After Husky snapped the heads off a couple of them, the Commander ordered him executed. Earl was supposed to do it. He smuggled the dog off Base and took him to his Mom's house. Then Ray told him about Dodo Bird getting killed so both of them being soft hearted, they decided my kids needed a new dog.

The snow was still really deep and when I saw Earl walking toward the house, leading a Shetland pony behind him, I didn't realize we were about to become the owners of a really large dog. This was the largest husky I had ever seen. He had been raised just to be a mascot and had the very best diet possible and trained to military precision. He weighed 185 pounds and was not fat. The kids adored him at first sight and he was wonderful with them.

This dog knew military commands. He could march, double time, attention, and whatever was barked out, he knew exactly what to do. He expected grooming and would bring his brush over, then stand so many seconds for each part, left, right, back, front.

If you snapped on his military leash, he came to attention. He always started out on the same foot. He was not trained for guard duty. Or if he was, Earl neglected to tell us the correct commands. We had to keep him tied as we didn't want a repeat of Dodo Bird. Toad had some stuff stored in the garage by the house and Husky would lay right there and watch people take things.

My parents sent us the money to come spend the Holidays, a couple of years after moving to Alaska. I went, fully intending on never coming back. After 2 days in Oregon, I was more than willing to come back and never leave Alaska again. I had conveniently forgotten the Toad's family. They still lived in Oregon.

Toad's idea of spending half the time with each family, was, nights were spent with my family and all waking hours with his. If you have never seen a family of screaming fighting toads, you've been very lucky. We went back to Alaska.

The people across the road had a horse that they fed trash from the grocery stores in town. They didn't even take the wrappers off the heads of lettuce. The horse was kept in a small corral, not enough room for exercise and her feet were terrible from standing in her own waste all the time. Why she survived I will never know. Then she had a foal. They left the baby and her in that filthy corral. Someone finally turned them in, I would have if I had a phone, and they had someone else come trim up her poor feet and started tying her out to feed along the road.

They bought a couple hundred baby chicks and turned them loose to free range. Those chickens drove Husky crazy and he would strain at the end of his chain, trying to catch one.

Finally, he figured out if he walked to the end of his chain, then backed up a few feet and laid down, the chickens would come closer to taunt him. This worked beautifully and he had at least one chicken a day the rest of that summer.

His surrounding area was a sea of white feathers. The chicken owner came over going to kill our dog. I did suggest if anything happened to the dog, he might wish it had not. Then I pointed out that my dog was tied and never loose and his chickens were ruining my garden and flower beds. He left, but not happily.

The weather started getting cold and they finally came and asked if I would show them how to butcher chickens. No one in their entire group had a clue. I told them I would tell them how to actually kill them, but I would not do the killing. They started killing chickens.

Then they came back as they could not figure out the directions on scalding, plucking and cutting up the chickens after they were dead. I ended up helping them do the entire flock and did not get one single piece of chicken for my efforts. Guess they figured the dog ate my share.

The landlord wanted to raise the rent. We asked that the place be repaired so we could actually use the whole little house and have running water. He saw no reason to. I started searching the newspaper.

I started loving the easy going lifestyle of Alaska. As long as you don't bother me, I won't bother you, should have been the State Motto. Now it has changed a lot and not for the better. People move up here to get away from it all, then spend the rest of their lives trying to make it "Just like home."

Chapter 13

I found a house a little bit out of North Pole on Laurance Road. They wanted to sell, but would allow the rent to go to the down payment plus $500 for the down within a year of renting. This sounded like as good a deal as we were ever going to find.

Toad still worked for the railroad. A personal record on a job at that time. We didn't have the $500 but I thought just maybe we could save it during the year we rented. Toad decided to start collecting more guns and found another girlfriend.

This one worked at the strip club, Telon's Too. He also started smoking weed. Neither helped save money for the house. Just before the deadline for purchasing or moving out, I asked my parents for a loan. They sent a check for the entire $500 as we didn't have a dollar saved toward the down. Never repaid, of course.

Then we went partners in a couple of pigs. The partners had the room for them, so they kept them and we supplied food for them. We butchered late in the autumn and I cured and smoked the hams and bacon. No smoke house, so I used our porch. The house certainly smelled good after that.

We were now the owners of a house on an acre plus a bit of ground. There were several lovely large spruce trees and some birch. A small area of willow looked like it would be a great garden area.

In the loan for the house was enough money to move the house and put a daylight basement under it. The kids would each have a bedroom and a large play area for when the weather was too rotten or cold for outside.

At present, the kids had the master bedroom as it was large and gave them room for playing and we had Willy, Sue and their kids quite often. Our bedroom was very small and we struggled setting up the double bed in it. The closet was along the entire wall with 2 doors, so we would go through the edge of the closet to get in and out of bed. Our covers and mattress froze to the outside wall.

Our first Thanksgiving in the house, before the basement was added, Willie, Sue and 4 kids came over for Thanksgiving dinner. They brought his mom, sister and 4 brothers. Sue's parents came also, but at least they went home after dinner. The rest stayed until Easter.

We finally went over and shoveled the road in to their house and hauled them all home.

With 12 extras living with us that winter, sleeping arrangements were tight. The kids all slept in the room our kids were in. The rest used the couch, chairs and the floor. One bathroom made it a necessity for the males to all go out in the woods to pee.

    Laundry was a nightmare. I had a washer, no dryer, so clothes were hung all over the house to dry. They had not brought spare clothes when they came to dinner, so they used ours and theirs was washed almost every night and hope they were dry by morning. The kids used our kids' clothes for school. The Toad left for work during the week and spent weekends partying with his girlfriend. Sometimes he, Ray and Willy hung out somewhere.

    One evening when they came in, I had just baked a huge batch of cookies. Toad picked up each cookie and licked one side and put them down. Ray looked at him, picked up each one and licked the other side. Willie said "screw it" and ate all he could hold. He got the entire batch. No one else would touch them.

    I got the check for our tax returns before the Toad knew it was due back and ordered a Troybilt rototiller. This was the horse model and I wanted to see if it really would do as well as advertised. I tilled up the willow patch. It took 4 times over it to chop up all the pieces of willows, but since they were taller than me, that was really good. I was going to have an excellent garden.

I also tilled up the area behind the house where it used to sit before being put on the new daylight basement. There were no rooms built yet downstairs, but the kids had marked out their areas, and moved their beds down there. We had lockers they used for closets.

I spent hours getting our garden in and taking care of it. We grew a wonderful garden that year and I was even able to can a lot for the coming winter. This was even with feeding all the extras we had at meals.

I was starting to believe we could make a go of it, keeping the family together until the kids were grown, anyway.

The Toad still ran around, still came home from running around and yelled at me for what he was doing. I was finally losing weight and losing a lot of it. My stomach refused food and would not digest. I could eat a tablespoon of food a day and not throw it back up. The doctor said it was my nerves and gave me pills. The pills relaxed me to the extent I felt like a zombie and totally distanced from what was going on around me. The doctor said as long as my situation remained the same, I would have the problem, as far as he could tell. I flushed the pills after the first day and lived with the nervous stomach.

I was doing some book keeping work for Earl's boss at the tire shop. I had started doing his billing while we lived over in the last house where we met Earl and Ray. Earl would drop off the books and billing supplies, I would make out the invoices and address the envelopes and Earl took them back in with him when he went in to work.

I finally met the man when he and Earl decided to go hunting but partway out, found they didn't have a rifle. They were both drinking fairly heavily and he was driving his old dump truck. They pulled in the yard, Earl came in to see if they could borrow a rifle. Toad loaned them mine.

Earl took it out to the truck and figured we should meet his boss. He introduced us and Charlie opened the door of the truck, and it swung wide open with him still clinging to it. Then it swung back and dropped him onto the seat. He got upright and they left, hunting. He quit drinking shortly after that.

He always sent cash out with Earl to pay for the book keeping. When we went to town, we sometimes stopped over at his tire shop and said Hi. He was in the middle of a nasty divorce, so wasn't very sociable. I would work in the office while the men talked out in the shop. Then we would go home or do whatever else we were in town for. My kids liked going there as he had a nice dog and they played with it. He also usually had a bowl of candy he let them demolish.

The Toad decided he wanted to make some of the big money to be made up north on the pipeline that was finally going in. The lawsuits were all settled and it was back to business as usual.

Fairbanks screwed themselves out of becoming the headquarters town for the big oil companies. Anchorage wasn't much bigger than Fairbanks at that time and completely off the pipeline corridor. However Anchorage was willing to cut some excellent deals with the oil companies for tax breaks and assorted other perks if they would move there. Fairbanks is always looking for the quick buck and raised the prices of everything and the oil companies deserted in droves. Fairbanks still does this.

Personally, I prefer Fairbanks as a much smaller town. I really dislike having to go to Anchorage for anything. It is just like any other large city anywhere else in the United States. Fairbanks still had delusions of grandeur and gutted the downtown of anything that ever made it interesting in favor of parking lots and hotels, regardless of the residents' votes.

So Toad quit the railroad and asked Charlie to get him a job up north. Charlie did. Toad would work one week, get a check, come home, spend it and then go back up to work on another job. He bought guns and cameras, the best of both. He stayed true to form, he didn't pay the bills. Our phone and electricity got shut off, Charlie bailed us out as it was winter. While Toad was working for the railroad, we opened a checking account and I kept the bills paid up. Now, he got the checks and cashed them. He and cash never did well for the family. He spent time with his girlfriend and their group had a cabin out at Harding Lake.

He would promise the kids that he was going to be home in time to take them places they wanted to go. He never actually did those things and stupid me, I made excuses for all his lapses in parenting. I was trying not to make the kids hate him as much as I was starting to and bent over making sure they did not know how I felt.

I never argued as he managed to always think he knew what I was thinking and carried on both sides, saying what he thought I was thinking, then his rebuttal. If he hadn't been serious, it would have been funny. He never once got my thoughts correct, yet he still swears he was right. After we split up, he claimed I never loved him as I would not fight with him. I never thought fighting showed love.

He claims I hated my son from the start. No, I loved my son and still do. I hated the way he was conceived which had nothing to do with him and he was not at fault. No matter how I look at it, I felt like he was conceived by rape. At the time, that was not a valid thought as a husband could do whatever he wanted to his wife. About a year later, a woman in Salem filed rape charges against her husband and it went to Court. She won, which changed the way it was handled from then on, at least in Oregon.

But, he kept telling our son I hated him, and he still believes his Dad. He says he has no memory of living with me. He now thinks it was me that used to duct tape him and hang him on the wall from a nail. Maybe someday he will remember the truth about it.

Finally, one night I almost committed murder. Toad promised the kids we would spend the weekend doing things just with them. Then he left and didn't come home until late Sunday night. He spent the weekend out at that lake cabin. He walked in the door and started yelling at me for screwing around on him. I think I possibly have never been as angry in my life. I actually had a red haze around my field of vision. My face must have shown a bit of what I was thinking and none of it was good. If he had opened his mouth just one more time to say any of that, I would have just shot him and to hell with the consequences. I had made excuses all weekend to our kids, they had cried themselves to sleep over his being gone and he pulls this?

Hind sight being 20/20, I should have kicked him out. Instead I yanked the pickup keys out of his hand and went out the door. I drove around and didn't know what to do. All our friends were his friends. I didn't have any.

I went to Fairbanks, everything was closed. I was driving up and down side streets all over town and getting low on gas with no money. There were lights on at Charlie's house. I stopped. Maybe I could get an advance on pay for doing his paperwork.

I tapped on the door and his daughter who was just getting home from work as night clerk at a hotel in town answered the door. She took me over to the front apartment which was empty and I spent the rest of the night there. Somewhere about 5 in the morning, I saw the Toad go by with one of his friends. Of course our pickup was right there, by Charlie's house so he imagined the very worst. The fact that Charlie had just got home from the hospital after a heart attack didn't matter, I must be in there with Charlie.

When I talked to Charlie the next morning, having learned some of the Toad's habits, I asked if I could rent his apartment. He wasn't thrilled but said yes. I went to an attorney. He filled out papers, but would not file anything until the divorce was paid in full. I started looking for a job.

While filling out paperwork at the hospital for work as a dishwasher, one of the cooks quit. It was while they were preparing lunch and lunch had to be served in less than an hour. I was hired as a cook. My shift started immediately. At that time, a cook was paid a flat $800 a month. After paying rent, I was hard pressed to get the attorney paid off fast enough to get the paperwork filed and in process. I ate at work. Charlie let me use the old work truck and I picked up one of the other kitchen helpers that lived near the apartment so they paid for the gas.

My kids didn't want to move in with me. Later I found out the Toad told them I would come back if they stayed with him and we would all be a family again and go do all the stuff he always promised them. They were 11 and 12 at the time. My always making excuses for him was coming back to bite me in the butt. They believed him.

Charlie was feeling better and got cleared to go back to work, so needed someone to stay with his kids. He had three teenagers. He would waive my rent if I would keep an eye on them and maybe fix meals now and then. That would speed up my divorce being filed, so I accepted.

He left for up north and when he was gone, I stayed on their side of the house. I cooked evening meals but the kids weren't use to having anyone there. Before their folks got divorced, as soon as Charlie left for work the wife took off and didn't come home until he was due home, several weeks later. Charlie hadn't known that until recently and that was when he filed for divorce. The woman asked for custody of the kids, but while drunk, she told the kids they would still live with their dad, she just wanted the child support and the money for selling the house, they would be in her way. The kids walked downtown to her attorneys' office and told him there was no way they would go with their mother, so he better change how the papers were being filed.

The attorney finally got her to agree to Charlie getting custody and keeping the house he built, she got the apartments he had built across the alleyway from the house. She was upset but her attorney told her if her kids told the Judge what they told him, she might not get the apartments, either. She caved.

Me, 1976
Just after my divorce

PART THREE – I FINALLY GET IT RIGHT (MAYBE)

Chapter 14

Toad got an attorney. I finally had the fee paid and my attorney filed the papers. Toad broke in to my apartment and was going to possibly beat on me, if the way he had me grabbed by my shirt and chest, feet dangling and his other fist drawn back was any indicator. That was when he talked himself out of it. He stormed back out of the apartment, slamming the ruined door.

When I got home from work a few nights later, Charlie was home from up north and working on the pickup, out back. He said I had a flower delivery, it was in his kitchen. I went on in and there was a small arrangement of flowers with an envelope on it. I opened the envelope and there was a letter from the Toad, telling me what an ungrateful bitch I was and he and the kids were gone and I would never see them again. I would be sorry as he was the best thing that ever happened in my life. Wow, I hoped not. I cried for my kids.

I drove out to the house and the phone was off the hook. It was still open on the other end. He had called his parents in Oregon and left the phone line open, trying to make sure I had a wonderful phone bill. He had not read his divorce papers very well. He got the bills until our divorce was final which wasn't for another 30 days. Every light in the house was on, the faucets all running. I went back to my attorney and had the papers changed to reflect the new circumstances.

The envelope on the floor explained how they traveled. Our joint federal tax return came in. He got one of his new lady friends to sign my name on it and while they were at it, they went to a car lot in town and traded in our pickup for a pretty, newer pickup, with her signing my name to the contract. She was driving the pickup.

The first I knew about the pickup was when the car dealer called about the late payment. They even used Charlie's phone number on the contract. The man was rather rude on the phone so I went over in person to see exactly what it was all about.

The woman with the Toad had evidently made an impression on the car dealer as he was expecting her to walk in. I walked in and he asked if he could help me. I said I had just spoke to him on the phone about a pickup he claimed I signed for. He got very flustered. He described the soon-to-be-ex-wife of a friend of ours. Short, heavy, quite pretty, loud, flirtatious. I told him if he wanted his truck, he ought to go looking for her as I had seen her driving it and it was rumored she was driving it in the races at North Pole.

She broke into my house at North Pole and killed one of my cats while she was in there going through everything, taking what she wanted and all the guns not already taken by the Toad. She took all except what I had with me in town, my handgun and my old military rifle I had since I was 12. She vandalized what she didn't take and later sent most of the stuff down to the Toad, she said.

He never admitted any of it. Several of the guns were mine, including the old 32-20 Marlin rifle my Dad had given me. It was the only thing he ever gave me and I loved that gun. That is probably the only reason the Toad took it. The front sight was a piece of a buffalo nickel. I turned it in as stolen, but nothing ever came of that.

After my final Court date, Charlie asked if I would like to spend the summer out at some mining claims he was half owner on. His partner was the kind man that allowed me to warm up at 26th Street Market the night I almost froze to death. Charlie was a good listener and nice to work with. No yelling at me nor calling me names. If he asked for an opinion, he actually listened while it was given. Sometimes even following my suggestions. How radical.

    I accepted and turned in my notice at the hospital. The shift there was killing me on lack of sleep. My shift started at 4:30 a.m. and ended at 1 p.m. No one went to sleep at Charlie's house until around midnight and the boy's bedroom was under my apartment. Maybe a quiet summer out of town would let me catch up on sleep.

Chapter 15

Charlie, his youngest son, their dog Dum-Dum and I drove out to look the mine over and see just what we would need for the summer. The 'highway' was all dirt except the first 10 miles of it. The remaining 122 miles was dirt and some gravel here and there. It was narrow and followed the contours of the land. Most of it was the same level as the surrounding scenery.

The big trucks were hauling pipe north on half of it, until we turned towards Manley. They owned the road, just ask one. They got much nicer as time passed. Then they got helpful, if we had a flat, they would stop and help. They had learned the locals were the only help they could expect along that road.

The scenery was spectacular in some areas. Ptarmigan Pass opens up and there is the entire Tanana River through the Minto Flats clear over to the Alaska Range. On clear days, there is Denali, high above everything. A totally beautiful scene that I never tire of. Then there is North Hill. Almost straight down on the north side of the road and very steep uphill on the south side of the road with no guard railing at all and super narrow.

Applegate Creek meanders way down at the bottom on its way to the Hutlinana. There is an unimproved natural hot spring up the Hutlinana with no road access.

The cabin was adorable, nestled in deep moss like it had grown there. Walking on that moss raised clouds of bugs, all hungry for blood. The cabin was 14'x20' and built in the 1930's. There was a very small room stuck on the back, made of boards. More of an afterthought to keep things dry that didn't matter if they froze or the bugs got in around them.

The front door was a screen door. That screen door was amazing. It was all that was used for over 30 years as a front door. It was very old, made out of wood with a screen portion where most have a window. The actual inside door was just boards nailed together but no latch or hasp on it and as the cabin settled, it was stuck in the open position and probably became part of the front wall support as the cabin is actually slowly falling down.

It was a lot too breezy with only the screen instead of glass, so we stapled cardboard from a stereo carton inside the door as partial insulation and to keep out most of the breezes as the wood pieces were rather wide apart, also. We used a hook and eye latch on the inside and a hasp and lock on the outside if we were gone. That was more to let folks know we were gone than to keep anyone out as the wood on both ends of the hasp was rotten.

We never had a problem with bears tearing into the door until a couple of years ago, one demolished it and trashed part of the inside of the cabin. Now the cabin has a handmade door but it isn't the same and has no character.

As soon as the small dozer was unloaded, Charlie scraped all the lovely yard away. By the time he did it, I agreed. It cut the bug population by over half. Most of the voles, too.

There was a very large, very rusty wood cookstove in the cabin to use as heat and cooking. When it was going, the flames flickering inside cast their glow on the walls and ceiling. The ceiling was made of peeled poles, placed side by side with newspapers and magazines on top, then birch bark on that for waterproofing and dirt on top of that. When anyone got too bored, they could use a flashlight and read some tidbits through the small space between poles. There was some old rusty sheets of corrugated metal on top of that, but the place leaked everywhere.

The suspected serial killer that used to live near 50 mile holed up in this cabin when he was hiding out from the police. He placed all the mattresses against the windows and kept a diary on paper plates. Some were still around on the floor.

There was a very old, very well used outhouse behind the cabin. That would be priority one. New outhouse. Then another layer of metal went on the roof, although there was nothing but dirt under it to nail to. We put heavy pieces of other assorted metal on top to hold the sheets down. Dozer pads were a favorite.

Then we started tilling up an area for a garden and found a lot of unusual pieces of metal that evidently had been carried over during the gold rush by someone that thought they really needed them for something or other. Some may have been parts for the dump mechanism used to dump the dirt drift mined out of little tunnels all winter to sluice during the summer. They were not very handy when hit with the rototiller. They did well holding down roofing metal.

Charlie's partner couldn't take the summer off from his store to come mine with us, so he hired Harvey to come work in his place. Harvey immediately claimed the double bed in the cabin. Oookay. Youngest son grabbed the twin bed by the door, used as a couch when there was company, as his bed.

We set up a mattress on the floor in the small back room. One night spent back there and we dragged the little bunk house down to the yard from up near an old trailer near the sluicebox. Years ago, a young man was killed and partially consumed by a black bear between his pickup and that old trailer.

It was a dinky little building, 7'x9' so not a lot of extra space. A box of clothes could be placed at the foot of the twin bed, there was a small closet/shelf unit built on one side and a table fastened to the wall across from it with the outer two legs on the floor and other two cut off. A very small chair was pushed against the table, if it were left pulled out, it was in the way.

A tiny wood stove that used to be called a trash burner was in the corner near the front door. The door was just cut out of the plywood the building was made of and some 1"x2" pieces fastened on it to give it an edge around it and keep it from warping too much. The building was painted light blue.

A hole was cut out in the upper center of the door and a piece of screen fastened over it for light and ventilation. That wasn't quite enough, so a hole was cut beside the table and a window set in. Now it had light inside. A piece of rug tossed on the floor to keep from getting slivers from the plywood and it was all set up.

Youngest son and I learned to operate dozer that summer. We learned on the little Case 310 which was small enough neither of us were intimidated by it.

Then Charlie and Harvey got the old HD-10 running and we started learning to operate it, too. It had a clutch shift lever on the far left hand side, the gear shift in the middle and the blade control lever of the far right. When I say far left or right side, I mean really far from each other. The seat was wide enough for three people to sit on it comfortably. Those levers would be simple to operate simultaneously if you were an Orangutan. Since none of us were, he sat on one side and operated the pedals and levers on that side and I sat on the other side, doing the same.

We only ran at one speed, wide open, so the throttle lever was set and forgot. It had steering clutches and brakes. We each were using the ones on our side of the dozer. We actually got pretty good at it.

The rabbits and voles were loving the garden. So we finally brought out metal posts and chicken wire. We only put a three foot high fence around it because anything but the little varmints could either just walk through or over any fence we tried making so figured make it short and maybe they wouldn't ruin it.

The moose just walked through while the calves picked up the row markers and carried them along in their mouths until they found another one. The bears took one bite out of each squash. Spit it out and go on to the next one. Anything red, yellow or white attracted the bears' curiosity but they ignored the green zucchini. They never ate any of the stuff, just took one big bite out of each one. Somehow I couldn't trim it up and eat the rest. A bear has horrible breath and the thought of eating something they mouthed just didn't appeal. I know, picky, right?

We set up rain gutters around the cabin roof and had a barrel on the garden side and a tank hung just under the rain gutter with a faucet on it, on the other side of the cabin. We built a small table and put a basin and soap and towel there for keeping hands washed. When no one was around, we used it for showers, also. Traffic was almost nil on that little back road. Road traffic we could hear coming a long ways away and the occasional low flying airplane was easily heard in time to get inside.

One day while there alone, I was finishing rinsing my hair and wrapping a towel around my head as I turned to go into the cabin, I saw feet. There were a pair of unfamiliar work boots, just visible under the edge of the towel. I hadn't considered pedestrians. Not something that usually wanders by 142 miles from town. I kept the towel around my head and over my face and walked right on by the feet, not acknowledging his presence. I figured he had already certainly seen the rest of me, but I didn't have to let him know I knew it. I went on into the cabin and did not look back out or try to see who it was, but we did build a shower house right after that.

Charlie still walked nude from the door of the cabin to take his showers until the day the new neighbor's sister and young son came to visit and went to the sound of running water in the shower house instead of to the cabin door. Don't know what they expected in a small building with the sound of running water, but I guess a naked Charlie wasn't it. They made a hasty retreat and never visited again.

Bill wanted us to drag his old Volkswagen bus over from a cabin and claim they used to own and get it off that property. We saw the man living on the claim and said we wanted to come get it. He said fine, he was using it to store dry dog food but would move it out. We went over one morning to see what would need done before we could pull it away.

We were in the old Ford crewcab pickup and the transmission didn't hold too well in Park, so I slid over and held the brakes while Charlie and Kenny looked over the bus.

My handgun had slid off the seat and was down near the door when the man walked down and looked me and the pickup all over. I think he was looking to see if we were armed. Charlie nor Kenny had any type of weapon. The bus had two flat tires, so they were bracing and jacking up the bus to take the tires in to repair. Kenny was using the star wrench to loosen lug nuts on the back tire while Charlie jacked up the front and used a crescent wrench to take lug nuts off with. The man Rob, his sidekick Tom, two strangers wearing guns, a photographer and a journalist from Europe all came running out of the house, coming down the hill toward us.

    I reached down and grabbed my handgun and tried to get Charlie's attention. The men came around both ends of the bus, yelling and screaming about claim jumpers, with their guns pulled out, waving them around. The guy that lived there jumped in front of Charlie which left Charlie's back to his young son. The other so-called tough bad man started taunting young son. He was trying to get back to the pickup and the man opened fire between his feet, into the rocks.

    I didn't know what to do. There were more men than I had bullets and that damn photographer was jumping around snapping pictures right in everyone's faces. The Journalist was taping and writing notes like crazy over to one side and I pretty much blamed them for this whole incident.

    When the gun went off behind Charlie, he reached down and grabbed the jack out from under the bus and had it in one hand and the crescent wrench in the other, every time Rob stepped back, Charlie stepped toward him as Rob had a reputation of either belly shooting people or pistol whipping them with his handgun he wore in a specially made holster across his middle. He could shoot it without drawing it.

His hand kept hovering around the grip but if he had touched it, Charlie would have clanged the jack and crescent wrench on each side of his head.

Then Rob looked over at me in the pickup and I had the .357 magnum resting on the dash, aimed right through the windshield at the middle of his buddy Tom's forehead. His buddy was still taunting stepson, Rob said something to him and when he looked up and his eyes registered exactly what he was seeing, he turned white as a sheet.

I would have pulled the trigger if the boy had cried out hurt or Charlie, either one. It could even have been from a rock chip, but I would have shot. I was afraid if I opened the door, they would all just focus on me and then I couldn't save anyone. I would have shot Tom first, then Rob, then that damn photographer and he would have been the one I would have gone to jail for, he was unarmed except with his tongue which he kept yelling at them for more. There would have been the other two men and the journalist and I would only have had two more bullets.

After seeing that I had a gun, Rob called off his minions and they all backed slowly up the hill. Charlie and son got back in the pickup and I slowly backed down the hill, watching them and trying not to back off into the creek. Right on the dam over the creek, the pickup ran out of gas. Talk about a tense little bit while Charlie poured some gas into the tank from the spare can we had in back. The gauge didn't work on the truck and we never left much in it as thieves in the area siphoned gas all the time. I expected rifle shots at any moment. Charlie drove from there.

I was shaking like a leaf by the time we got back to the cabin. I don't think I have ever been that scared before. At that time, Charlie and I had been married just over two weeks.

We went down to Baker Creek and visited with Mr. Albert, the man that lived there at that time. He had a little cabin and a lovely garden and greenhouse. We were all talking about assorted stuff and I was still shaky, so told him about how close I had come to shooting as many of those people as I had bullets for.

I don't know whether or not he talked to them that evening, but about midnight that night, Tom woke up a neighbor near him and signed over everything he claimed in the area, then left the State. It was rumored that he shot a policeman in Nevada and spent some time in jail. A real pillar of any community. Sometime later, the Volkswagen bus appeared with the tires repaired, parked over near our cabin.

A few weeks later, our house in town was badly damaged by a fire. The kids and my brother were celebrating their birthdays with a three day party and somehow a cigarette fell into upholstery, wasn't noticed, everyone went to bed and it smoldered until many hours later it flared into life and gutted the upstairs, at least that's what we think.

We got a message on Trapline Chatter (a radio program to send messages to people in the Bush without phones) "There's been a small fire, mostly smoke damage, suggest you come home."

Charlie and I headed straight for home, even though it was already 9:30 p.m. and got home shortly before midnight.

We pulled in the back alley where we usually parked and looked at the house in disbelief. All the windows were missing with black smoke residue up the walls from each window. Looking into the house, everything was black. We didn't say a word to each other and went around to the front of the house which was a separate apartment. No damage showed at all from the front. There were no kids in sight or anywhere around the house. They knew enough to be keeping a very low profile as they were not supposed to party and had assured us they could be responsible young adults.

The front door wasn't locked, so we went on in and got a few hours of sleep. Then we called the insurance company. The man came right over, but the kids, trying to lessen the impact of the mess had pitched all the furniture and belongings out one of the windows into a pickup and hauled it all to the dump. All the adjuster was seeing was a bare bunch of rooms, charcoal coated and colored. There was nothing to look at to measure our loss of possessions.

They had left the fridge and stove and on top the fridge was my sketch book of lampblack paintings that I was filling up toward a show I had been promised at The Art Gallery downtown. Since I had a base price for my work through past sales, the loss of these pictures was established and that was pretty much all the possessions we were paid for. They paid about ten cents on the dollar for estimated furniture and personal belongings based on a minimum they set since nothing was there to actually see.

The two boys and my brother trickled back to the house several days after the fire. Cindy was staying in California at the time.

Charlie had built the house as one large room, sheet rocked it and then added walls where he wanted them so none of the interior walls were load bearing. We decided to change the rooms around a bit so tore out most of the walls and put up a few new ones. The sheetrock had saved the building, structurally. We tried everything people suggested to clean the smoke off the walls and ceilings. Finally we just used oven cleaner, the kind sprayed in a cold oven, then rinsed off. That stuff removed the smoke damage right down to the paint and if left on too long, on through to the sheet rock.

A man we had met the summer before out near the mine came by to see if he and his neighbor could stay at our place while looking for enough work to buy groceries for the winter for their two families out near Rampart. We told them they were welcome, but the facilities were not in great shape as we were sleeping on the floor in sleeping bags and eating whatever we had growing in the garden. Every penny was going into getting the house enclosed before winter hit. They said fine, and moved in.

The tomatoes and onions were producing extremely well so were featured in most of our meals. It was many years later before the man told us he actually never could eat either vegetable before and had not liked them, but after having so many weeks of only that as part of each meal, he now liked them and could eat them. I felt bad for not even asking if anyone had food problems. They did day labor at various places around town and if we were working on things after dinner in the evening, they helped out when they could, then too. We were able to buy them each a large turkey to take home for their families for Thanksgiving, with all the trimmings.

Every bit helped and we did not freeze that winter. By Christmas, the house had a couple of dumpster couches in the freshly painted living room. Charlie's brother and family that lived near Fairbanks came for Christmas dinner with us. All the kids were home, the house was enclosed and warm. It was a good Christmas.

Charlie and I at the mining cabin, part of the shower house showing at extreme right. This was right after I burned off part of my hair.

Chapter 16

    Charlie's Mom had come up to visit shortly before we got married. She was afraid Charlie was doing to his kids exactly like her Dad did to her as a child. He married a royal bitch that made her life hell until she ran away from home at age 15 to earn a living by herself. I didn't know why she had come, but I loved getting to know her. She spent a week with us, then a week with her other son and family that lived near Fairbanks, then came back and spent another week with us. Just before she left, she told Charlie he better hurry up and marry me, then she told me why she had come. I felt honored that she liked me.

    A couple of years later, we went to upstate New York and visited with her a couple of weeks. I need to brush up on social skills. The first people we met after starting the rounds of visiting his family asked me how I liked the mountains. I said I loved mountains but we had not had time to go see any yet. Charlie nudged me. We were in the mountains, they consider the Adirondacks, mountains. I didn't think we had seen any mountains once we were east of the Rockies. Oops. Nothing like getting off on the right foot for me.

I did have a lovely time there and the area was certainly full of rugged rock outcroppings and waterfalls. It was late September and the colors were just getting started on the tree foliage which was very pretty. I loved the huge old maple trees in the sugar orchards. We even went to Lake Placid and saw the Lipizzaner stallions perform. I thought it was odd that for the Winter Olympics, they had to build an artificial hill for the ski jumps as there were no hills high enough, so much for mountains.

We also spent a week in New York City and that was enough to last me a lifetime. It was interesting and we did lots of things tourists are told to never do and managed to survive and not even get mugged. We also took some tours to see all the tourist attractions as a week would probably not have been long enough to see them all on our own. We managed a show at Radio City Music Hall and cheesecake at Lindy's on our own.

For Mother's Day one year, Charlie bought an HD-21 dozer at auction and gave it to me as a present. That was some Mother's Day present. While building road to the Homesite, the dozer spun around on some trees and one of the tall trees smacked me on top the head. I thought my spine was broken and my head, too, but neither was.

Another year, he gave me a Dodge 4x4 crewcab pickup with a gooseneck triple axel grain haul trailer with a dump bed for my birthday. None of these were new, but they were new to me. No one had ever done anything remotely similar and none have, since.

My best present was having my daughter get to come back and live with us. Something about her dad telling her to move the car and she did, from Oregon to Kansas. My son still wanted to live with his dad, so stayed in Oregon. That was a disappointment.

The big trailer was lost after Charlie died, when two guys that each claimed they loved me both neglected to pull it out to my property as they had pickups with the gooseneck hitch in the bed and my pickup was broken down and someone has since stolen the motor out of it. How difficult would it have been for either one to hook it up and pull it out here? Quite a difference in how men show they love someone. They only had two years to do it in, too.

I'll never forget Dum-Dum and eggs. He used to grab any egg he found and run with it to eat when he knew we couldn't get it first. He preferred them boiled, but raw was fine, also. I found a dozen eggs pushed back in a cabinet at the cabin that had been there many months so set the carton out to carefully dispose of, when he saw it. He sneaked the lid up and carefully picked up one egg and ran with it. He was gone a long time, then came back and carefully picked up another egg, went just out of the cabin and started digging a huge hole, carefully placed the egg into it and did the same with each of the remaining eggs. He never touched another egg to eat.

Charlie got hired for a temporary job at the Naval Research Laboratory at Barrow, Alaska. He headed the rebuild/overhaul of one of their turbines in the power plant. They offered him a permanent job, but he refused as he had a home and family in Fairbanks and didn't want to be gone 6 months at a time. Instead, by accepting the temporary job, the company made the regular crew rotate on vacations to keep Charlie there as temporary fill in for one of them all the time and it worked out to be an almost permanent job that way. They let him have me come visit any time we could manage it, so I got to visit Barrow quite often.

What a difference from sneaking into all the other camps, such as Prudhoe Bay where I pretended to be a new worker and managed an entire weeks' visit without getting caught. Twice. I did get kicked out of one of the camps just north of the Yukon River Bridge, as someone saw me that knew me. Oops.

My first visit to Barrow was midsummer. We landed and walked over to the terminal. The foremen of the Research Lab was there to give me a ride out to the station. My first impression was, "I see the dump, where is town?" (It has changed a lot since then.)

At that time, Barrow had above ground utilidors for natural gas utilities in part of town and they arched over the streets at the intersections. There were still only honey buckets, even on most of the Naval Base. The truck drove around town picking them up and dropping off empty buckets to place in the little wooden cabinets used to cover them. The bags were taken to the lagoon and dropped off.

The Naval Arctic Research Laboratory was a few miles out of town. We passed gas wells once in a while on the trip out. Someone had to drive around once an hour and press the button to inject antifreeze into the wells to keep them working. There had been 19 working wells around Barrow but it was down to only a few still working because they had a hard time finding someone that would be reliable about injecting the wells. Once they froze, they were finished.

My first trip up to Barrow, Charlie was living in one of the small Quonset huts set out in rows along streets on the Base. They had made everyone else take vacation time so we had the hut to ourselves for my week long stay.

The mess hall was another larger Quonset hut closer to the beach. The cook had been the chef at the American Embassy in Korea for many years and was a magnificent cook. His meals were works of art.

If I complimented him on anything, he made sure it was available at any meal I wanted it at. He even remembered from trip to trip and made my favorite foods whenever I visited. I guess Charlie and I were the only ones that ever told him thank you and complimented him on the food. Once he found that Charlie needed a certain diet, he got it.

Even before I left for home, the head Boss asked me to go to work for them. He offered a very good wage. I asked what the job would be doing. He said it didn't matter, they wanted Charlie to work there and figured if they hired me, he would stay. They renewed the offer every time I visited.

My next visit was around Christmas. As we landed, coming in, there were vehicles lined up side by side as close together as they could park and headlights lighting our way to the terminal from the plane. There were polar bears in town and near the airport.

The airlines didn't want anyone getting picked off between the plane and the door. By then they were phasing out using the Quonset huts as housing and everyone had rooms over in the huge lab complex. This was a very modern building that had running water and flush toilets instead of the honey bucket system. The mess hall was still in the large old Quonset, though.

Charlie had a friend purchase a 30-06 rifle with scope to give me for Christmas. They had shipped it up before I got there.

I was allowed into the animal research area and took pictures of the polar bear and the wolves. The bear was very friendly and loved to play with the broom, so the handler kept him occupied with the broom while I took pictures all around him. He could reach through the cage at any point and touch the outside walls.

Not really set up for visitors. He went to the Boston zoo when the Lab closed. He had lived his entire life with people and could not survive in the wild. The wolves were not as friendly, but still too habituated to people so homes were found for them, also.

The entire complex and Base made a huge deal out of Christmas. By this time, the sun had not been showing above the horizon for quite a while and anything as diversion was appreciated. The sun traveled just below the horizon during the middle of the day, so it isn't completely dark, just a bright combo sunrise/sunset as the sun never quite makes it over the far distant bumps of hills.

It looks flat around Barrow, but that is misleading. There are gullies. The vegetation down in the gullies may grow much taller than up on the tops, but then the wind hits the tops and it never grows beyond that. A person can walk along the ridges and not notice the land is deeply cut right beside them until they misstep down into it.

The wind wears the snow out in the winter. First it blows from east to west and all the snow is blown along, only being stopped by some protuberance, a rock, a blade of grass, a twig, and then it can make a huge drift building up from that minor obstruction. Then it changes and blows from west to east and all the snow gets moved back the other way. It is pretty ratty looking stuff by spring. It is never the fluffy easily packed stuff kids make snowballs and snowmen out of. There is very little moisture in it.

Charlie finally told the boss that he just could not keep working up there like that. He had a home and he would like to actually live in it. We had plans to mine again that summer.

Chapter 17

Just after we opened the cabin up and started setting up for our summer of mining, the Union contacted Charlie to go to work up North again on another short temporary job. He really didn't want to go, but if he refused a job when offered, he would not be getting the jobs he liked or enjoyed when he wanted one. He went.

We wanted to pick up and use some old pipe up along one of the hills. We asked our close neighbors that knew the people the pipe belonged to about it. They contacted the owners and we were given permission to take the pipe.

I had surgery a couple of months earlier and wasn't up to 100% feeling fine but before Charlie left for work, we picked up a couple of miles of 24 inch diameter 16 feet long steel pipe from one of the old ditches. The pipe was almost half buried and partially full of animal droppings. Those things were heavy. Slight hint here, if you have just had a hysterectomy, don't do this.

Everyone in the area must have been waiting for someone else to do all that work as the pipe started disappearing as soon as we had it piled. People took it to use as culverts and whatever else they figured they needed it for, I guess. We did get to use a few pieces, but after all that hard work, it was rather discouraging.

The folks that lived just above us on the same road were very nice. It took a little while to get acquainted as my people skills are a bit lacking and they were used to seeing fly-by-night would-be Miners come and go. By our second year out there, they were friends and we got along great.

Claire came to Alaska as a teacher for the town of Chicken many years ago, taking over from 'Tisha when she no longer taught there. After teaching at Chicken a while, she taught at Manley Hot Springs where she met Archie. Archie contracted hauling freight from the river at Manley to the mining claims located around Eureka, north of Manley.

Instead of the added expense of dogs or horses, Archie used his own muscle to haul the loads contracted for. Claire and Archie married and Claire had to give up her teaching as married women were not allowed to teach. Archie and Claire still worked their mining claims when I met them and did, until the summer of 1987. That was their last summer mining. They had sold their mining claims but retained ownership of their cabin in Manley.

She gave me her old treadle sewing machine. As they were packing their pickup to drive north from Washington State in early summer, 1988, Claire suffered a fatal heart attack. Archie never recovered from her loss and died in January 1989.

I really enjoyed all the old time Miners in the area. There was Archie and Claire that I looked up to and they were like having a wonderful set of Grandparents living nearby.

There was Tony, a nice man the same age as Archie. He lived and worked by himself over on a claim on the lower road past our cabin. He sold the Dinsmore cabin to Charlie years before. He and his wife raised two children for many years in that cabin.

A bit closer was Lloyd Hubbard, he was a retired DOT man that used to maintain the roads in the Manley Area. He loved to have anyone stop by and visit, he claimed that he did not retire to overwork now and would shut down his entire operation to come visit if he saw a vehicle on the road.

There was also the Martin Ott family. Martin worked by himself several years, but whenever his wife, Martha, had vacation time from working at J. C. Penneys, she came out and stayed. His youngest son worked with him a lot, also and now works their claims with his wife and family.

These people had all lived in Alaska for most of their lives. Some now left for the winter as they were semi-retired and only worked summers, mining.

There were other people that came up and mined during the summers, but they didn't actually live in Alaska and for the most part, never had.

There were also a few homesteaders as now homesteading was closed and only the ones that had filed just before the end of it were able to still claim land through the Homestead Act. Not all claimed land under the homestead provision. Some used the Trade and Manufacturing Site section and that was an excellent choice for this part of Alaska.

A couple of the families that filed under the Homestead section came up from Florida, saw a valley with only low growing vegetation, thought someone else had cleared it then dropped out so they hurried up and filed on it, thinking to profit by someone else's work. It wasn't cleared land, it was permafrost land. When the surface vegetation was scraped off or broken through by driving over it, it became bog. There was a hiking trail along the hillside that was on firm ground, but the winter trail in the valley could swallow vehicles whole, in summer.

One family that claimed land under the Trade and Manufacturing provision had to file in the wife's name as her sister had filed a paper claim under the husband's name on a parcel over on the other side of the hill that was mostly mining ground which was illegal to file on. Only one filing was allowed per person, regardless, so the land they eventually found was filed in her name. Charlie loaned them our little dozer for a while.

All the locals were a little leery about getting friendly with the Homesteaders. Too many of the la-la land hippies had come through already, all intent on living off the land with no clue what they would have to do to actually 'live off the land'.

Most of them ended up either stealing out of the Miners sluice boxes or just plain stealing. One family built a cabin that birds could have flown through the walls. They had two small children and were determined they would live there year around. Some time during the winter, they hiked out. No one heard from them again or anything about them so there was always the possibility that they did not survive the trip.

The main road to Fairbanks was not kept open in the winter at that time. Vehicles had to be left parked in a gravel pit near the turnoff to Minto, many miles away. One family made it, of all the people that filed. Years later, the BLM went ahead and gave 5 acres to each of the ones that filed homesteads. I am not too sure why, other than just for having tried.

One family filed homesteads in their name and in each of their adult son's names along the main creek on the mining side of the hill. They even used mining claim corners as their location corners. All of this was totally against the Law.

They kept turning in photos of lovely grain fields they had cleared and homes they had built and all the other improvements made on the land. The home office almost granted them the entire 160 acres each just on the photos alone.

The fly in their ointment was my husbands' brother. He was the field investigator for the BLM at that time and was familiar with the area they had staked in, since it was near our claims.

The narrow little canyon they staked for their sons certainly did not have room for the wide level fields of grain showing in the photos turned in. He had flown over the area only a few days before and all he saw was a couple of little shacks and a flourishing chop shop for cars.

He suggested the head man in the office drive out with him to visit these fine upstanding citizens. After their drop in visit, their main claims for patent on their assorted homesteads were denied, but they still were allowed 5 acres for the area around their cabin. The chop shop continued to flourish.

Later, one of the sons tried to race a landing airplane with a snowmachine and lost. He also lost his head, neck and shoulder to the prop.

Those sons would steal anything, even if there was no use for it to them. We used to leave an old HD- 10 dozer sit at Boston Creek for residents to use in the spring during breakup to make a path across the ice and drive across.

We came around the corner one day and there was one of the men up on the dozer, taking all the instruments off the dash panel. He had all the tiny screws out of the gauges and some of the gauges on the deck. When he saw us, he jumped over the hydraulics on the side and fell over the track to the ground, jumped on his motorcycle and started running and trying to start the motor as he ran down through the creek. I wish I had been able to video that.

Many years later, their houses, sheds and shop all burned down, what a shame. We always figured someone just finally got sick and tired of having to replace things those thieves had stolen. How they managed to find them all gone at the same time is amazing as usually they always made sure at least one person was home. I guess they were afraid someone might steal something back.

One of the other Federal land disposals was a program of Homesites. These were limited to 5 acres each, one per family. Most of the land available was on top of mountains or down in swamps. Usually there was no access to any of these and it would be up to the individual to figure out how they were going to get in and out. Of everyone I ever heard of filing on one of these, only one couple ever managed to find an area suitable for living on. They did finally get title to it, also. Then he took up mining and she took up mechanics and kept the equipment running for him. A perfect partnership.

Charlie and Bill, setting up near the mouth of Boston Creek.

Chapter 18

   Many years ago, it was illegal to leave a hitchhiker stranded, without at least offering a ride. After the population changed attitudes and values and people were getting robbed or murdered, the law was removed from the books. But it was still hard for me to pass a hitchhiker in remote areas of the road system without at least stopping and making the offer of a ride.
   So, when driving back from closing our mining camp, late in the Autumn on a road that was not maintained year around and seeing a person by the side of the road, I slowed down to stop.   Light snow was falling and the wind was blowing it around in swirls on the roadbed as I came across the high tundra above the Minto Flats far below. I had not seen another vehicle all day and the road would close if this snow continued. The fellow far ahead had jumped down out of the road grader parked off the edge of the road, so I assumed he was the operator. (I know, I know, 'assumed')

For some reason, I put my handgun on my lap under my jacket and held it in my left hand when I stopped to offer assistance.

The fellow jumped in my old pickup and was shivering badly, not dressed for the weather, wearing a light jacket, no hat, no gloves and no warm boots, just shoes. I was just about to let my handgun rest in my lap, to make shifting gears easier, when he slid across the seat until his knee was pressed against my thigh and one hand was on the seat back, touching the back of my neck.

I kept the gun in hand and shifted awkwardly but trying not to show how scared I suddenly was. He started fiddling with my hair and asked me if I was ever afraid of getting raped. I pulled my gun up, cocking it as I raised it, aimed directly at him and said, "Not really."

I thought the man was going to go right through my door he slid back across the seat so fast. I was driving at a fairly good speed by now and he hugged the door for the next 25 miles, until we reached the turn off for Livengood. I held the gun on him the entire 25 miles, he kept his mouth shut and hugged the door. The gun had a hair trigger, so if one bump or rattle went wrong, this story would have had a different ending. When I slowed down at the turn, he had the door open and didn't even wait for me to completely stop, he bailed out.

If that was supposed to be a pick up line, it was lame. If he actually had intentions to follow through, I have no idea. But since he had not actually done anything but touch me and say something inappropriate and stupid, I had no evidence to turn him in to the Troopers in town. At that time, having a concealed weapon was illegal, so I would probably have been the one in trouble.

Years later, I did get in trouble for a concealed weapon and it was by accident. One of the couples that used to drive up from Idaho and mine near us each summer had finally had to quit. He had Alzheimer's and got violent so she had to put him in a home. She came up for one last trip to say goodbye to all her friends from all the years they spent in Alaska. I drove her around and we went out to Eureka/Manley and stopped to visit everyone. We were fairly late getting back to the house in town and hurried up trying to get a bit of sleep. When we went out early in the morning to get to the airport for her early flight, the pickup had a flat tire.

We hurriedly transferred her luggage to my little Nissan and headed for the airport. I parked out at the curb and hustled her in through the doors and got her ticket taken care of. Then I almost carried her up the stairs to the security scanners. I remembered the tools in my coat pocket so took off my coat and dropped it on the floor and got her right on through security and to the gate she needed as they were closed the gate.

The stewardess reopened and called the plane to let them know another passenger was on her way down the ramp.

When I got back to the security check and started to leave, they said we have a problem. They had my jacket on the aircraft side of the scanner. There were not only tools in the pockets, but a small double barreled derringer. Since I occasionally carried gold to town for some of the other Miners, someone had given me the derringer as protection. I had promptly forgot it.

They escorted me to a small room and left me sitting there for quite a while. Finally a policeman came in and sat down. He asked me some questions and found out my husband was Charlie Stowell. The policeman used to live close to Charlie while growing up and Charlie would let him go fishing with him. He told me they could not just drop the whole thing, but to go on home and he would see what he could do. A few days later, I got a ticket in the mail, then I got a Court date. The policeman came by the house and tried to tell me what to expect in Court. He said I would probably get a fine as the Feds would also check out the ticket and if the State didn't do anything, the Feds would step in and also charge me.

I appeared in Court and pleaded no contest. The Judge said I needed an attorney and should not plead no contest as this was a serious charge.

I told him I knew it was serious, but why waste the Court's time and rack up expenses for something I had done? He said since I wasn't represented, he would have to advise me and that he advised me to plead innocent and get a good attorney. I told him what had happened. He said Case dismissed and give me back my gun.

The District Attorney bounced up and protested. The Judge asked her why. She said that even though she had no idea who I was and as far as she knew, we were not related, but her last name was also Stowell and anyone reading the record would assume I received special consideration. Then I jumped in and said if I got off with no sentence, the Feds would pounce on me saying the State wasn't doing its' job. The Judge got a little testy.

He said "So the Feds are waiting to get you if we don't give you some sort of sentence and you can't get your gun back or the State will think you are a relative of the DA? Sounds like threats to me, but just for the Record, $25 fine and try to stay out of trouble for a year. As a bit of advice, get a larger caliber gun for self-defense."

Evidently the Feds didn't think that was a harsh enough sentence and sent me a very obnoxious letter telling me I was under investigation and what the probable fines and jail time was going to be for my dangerous activities. They had a full year to bring charges. Every couple of months, they would send me another letter, scaring me half to death. The possible fine would have assured that I would lose my home and everything I owned. The jail time was impressive. People kill people and get less time.

Finally, almost a year from the first letter, I received another letter telling me to appear in front of them at a special room at the airport to hear my fate.

I went to the airport and found parking for long term, not knowing how long this might take. I finally located the room, a fairly large room with no windows that I didn't know existed in the airport complex. I knocked on the closed door and a man opened the door. There were several men in dark suits in the room, a large table with chairs all around it and they told me to sit. I sat.

We waited and waited. I made sure I didn't fidget or whine. Finally one of the men checked out in the hallway again and came back in. The others looked at him, then looked at me. All but one seat was taken and it was right beside me.

One of the men finally asked me just how long it would be before my attorney put in an appearance. I told them I didn't have an attorney. All the men immediately hurried to the other end of the room and huddled like football players dressed in suits. Finally one came over and sat down by me.

The man at the head of the table stood up and began reading off a list of charges they had decided to bring against me.

When he got to "attempting to bring a loaded concealed firearm into a secure area" on the first page of a multipage document, I raised my hand. The man beside me said to wait, he would answer the complaint after the man finished reading the entire complaint. Then he said he had been appointed to represent me since I did not have an attorney of my own. I told him thanks, but I needed to answer this one complaint right now as it was being read as evidently the people that wrote the complaint had not read the original documents.

Everyone looked at each other and started scrambling for copies. The man that had been reading asked what I meant. I told him I was not attempting to enter the secure area. I was attempting to leave the secure area when stopped and held.

The man that had been reading the charges found the correct document first and read it. He got a bit red in the face, slammed the entire list of charges down and started complaining about all of them having flown in from Washington D.C. for nothing. If anyone had paid attention, they would have noticed that one little detail.

Charges dismissed and sorry about this, you are excused. The fellow beside me patted my shoulder, said I was an unusual client and congratulations. The relief that went through me was almost enough to make me sick. For an entire year, these men had been threatening me with horrible consequences and now it was over?

The man beside me told me to keep breathing and not faint on them now. He handed me a glass of water, told me to sip on it a bit and then he would escort me out to my car. I did and he did. He looked surprised to see my ratty old pickup that I treasured, but never said a word. The snow plow was still on the front and the back seat was full of tools and winter gear. He shook his head, then told me he just could not imagine living in a situation that required any of these things. That was it. My year of worry and tension was over.

Chapter 19

Life with Charlie was certainly different than anything I had ever experienced before. A man that actually listened to a woman when she had an opinion and discussed options with her was nothing I had experience with.

His daughter was living and working in Hawaii. When she finally wrote and told us she was pregnant, he just about hit the roof. Then we talked it over and he finally calmed down enough to not immediately drive to town and call her to disown her. He finally understood that she was still his daughter and loved him as he loved her and this was just something that had happened. It was okay to keep loving her and to accept her child. This he did with complete acceptance and I was proud of him. A few months after the boy was born, she came home with him.

He was an adorable little guy. Her boyfriend was planning a huge drunken brawl of a first birthday party for him that she would be expected to pay for and she finally had enough. From knocking her down a flight of stairs when he found out she was pregnant in the hopes of making her lose the child, it was now HIS son. She was his meal ticket so he could continue to play on the beach and gamble with his friends and she worked full time to pay for it all and help out his family, also.

In order to come home, she had snuck down to the beach with the boy and then hiked until she could catch a cab and make it to the airport. She had no clothes for either of them, they still had beach sand on them from her running away. She moved into the front apartment of the house in town. It was a nice two bedroom apartment that was not quite finished, but comfortable even without the kitchen being done.

The first time her boyfriend called from Hawaii, he was fairly nice on the phone and asked if she was there and okay. Once he found out that she was, he became a loud demanding jerk. He would call at 2 or 3 a.m. and demand that we get up, get dressed warmly and go over and wake her up to come talk to him. By this time she had a job and her shift started in a few hours, she needed her sleep and I was not particularly happy about the calls. This was in deep winter and it could be under minus 40 degrees outside, he didn't care. We were supposed to go get her.

Then he demanded that she be back by the boy's birthday and she was to bring back 200 pounds of king crab, 200 pounds of salmon and 200 pounds of halibut, since she was in Alaska anyway, to serve their guests at the party. Of course she was supposed to figure out how to pay for all of this as he wasn't about to contribute. I don't know what he told all his buddies when that huge party didn't happen, but I was quite proud of her for sticking to her guns and not caving and going back to him at that time.

He lost their home, her car and all her possessions in one way or another. The car ran out of gas and he walked off and left it. What a sweetheart.

Several years later, she made him prove he actually was a responsible adult. He had to get and hold a job a year, stop drinking, stop gambling and she would come visit and see how it went from there. Evidently, it went quite well. They ended up getting married and had a little girl.

The boys were dabbling in marijuana. At that time, it was not exactly illegal in Alaska and they were still teenagers so I guess they figured they would not get a record for the rest of their lives if caught. We came in from the mine one time to find they had taken everything out of a bedroom in the basement, hauled in soil, put up grow lights and had a regular little farm going down there.

To say that Charlie wasn't happy was putting it mild. We left for a while and when we returned, the basement was returned to its usual condition. How they got all that dirt cleaned off the floor and the furniture back in, I don't know.

Then the oldest boy got a girlfriend that was a real gem. She used their product and spent the cash they had on hand to pay their supplier and took off. Of course the boys didn't clue us in on their money making efforts so one night when I happened to have spent the night in town at the house, I woke up to the sound of our front door sneaking open. Now if the person had just opened it and walked in normally, I would probably have slept through the entire thing, but sneaking wakes me up every time.

I knew it was a stranger because of the sneaking, so eased the revolver up and cocked the hammer. A scared sounding voice from the other room called, "Don't shoot, I'm leaving". The sound of footsteps running for the door and the door slamming were next.

Youngest stepson woke up in time to hear part of this. He had been asleep on the couch in the living room and raised up, just his eyes peeking over the top of the couch. "Thanks, Mom, you probably just saved my life."

We talked for a while and he admitted what he had been doing. I asked him if he planned on that as a way of life for the rest of his life and if he enjoyed knowing he had people wanting to kill him. He said he would stop and find another line of work. He left for the Lower 48 that morning and stayed Outside for quite a few years after that. I hope he really did change his way of making a living.

Then my daughter told me she was having a baby. After already going through all the anger at his daughter over this, Charlie took it rather well. He did tell her we would not babysit or take care of the child.

She worked every job she could and prepaid the hospital and doctor before giving birth. The last couple of months she spent with me, at the mine. At first, in one of the trailers, then in the cabin with me.

We had numerous bears that summer. There were 6 different bears that we saw, at the cabin, within a 5 day period. One finally had to be shot. He stayed around the cabin for 3 days, never quite in sight, but always pacing through the brush near us. My daughter was 8 ½ months pregnant by that time and staying with me in the cabin after the bears started showing up. Every time we left the cabin, whether it was to work, to the garden or to the outhouse, he was there.

The sound of his teeth clicking together was an unnerving accompaniment as we walked. Never out where we could get a clear shot, though. We tried yelling and firing shots in the air, that bear would not leave. Finally, one morning about 4 a.m., the blind cat jumped on my daughter on the couch and woke her up. The bear was in front of the cabin on the road. Both pulled my covers off, to wake me. If they were going to be scared, I could be awake and share it with them.

We turned the radio up full volume and the bear started for the door. I don't know if he didn't like our choice of station or what, but his fur raised and his teeth were clicking. I started to open the door to shoot him, my daughter was getting a bit more than excited and I thought we were going to have a home birth, right then and there. So I shot the bear through the screen door.

Our cabin is 14' x 20' and with the door closed, the sound of the pistol was something else. The cat hated me for hours until she could hear again. The door is a false sense of security at best, being an old rotten screen held together with cardboard to keep the breezes and some squirrels out.

We did have some grizzlies that came by every 6 days on their circuit, but they never bothered anything and although they scared me, they never acted threatening. I did get some very good pictures of them through the windows.

A couple of years earlier, one neighbor had been shooting bears all summer and I asked him if he would let us have one for sausage. He said he would. One morning, he woke us up, he had a dead bear in the back of his pickup, and did we still want one? We said" Sure" and he dumped it by the cabin.

My daughter and I dressed and were just started skinning when the neighbor was back. Do you want another bear? We said "Why not?" When he was walking back down to his cabin, another bear ran around the corner and almost ran into him. He shot it.

We skinned out both bears, her first time skinning anything, and quartered them. We spread clean sheets on the backseat of my old crewcab and loaded the meat, salted the hides, rolled them and put them in the back of the truck and headed for town.

Charlie was working at Pump Station 7 at that time, setting up the power house. In camp, the men had a habit of starting rumors in the morning and see if they could recognize their own rumors that evening.

That very morning, Charlie told the group at his table that I had woke up in the night to see a bear in the cabin by the stove and shot it from bed, then as I started to get up another one came through the back door and I jumped up on the bed and shot it as it ran by. No one questioned how he knew all of this, as there were no phones or radio between our areas. They just laughed and said "Sure, Charlie", as they knew I did mine on out the road another 80 or so miles.

Before noon, I pulled up at the gate where the security guard was stationed to have him let Charlie know I would be at home that night. He looked down into my pickup from his perch and spotted the hides in back and the fresh meat in the backseat. His eyes got a little bugged out and he asked what I had. I told him, "A couple of bears".

That man didn't even wait to let someone take his seat in the guard shack, he took off running down the hill into camp, yelling, "It's true, it's true."

By the time Charlie came home that evening, I had all the meat ground up and in three piles on the counter and was working different spices into each pile. I made summer sausage, pepperoni and salami. Charlie eyed the meat but didn't say anything.

The next morning, I took him out to work and as I was coming home, the rest of the crew were honking and waving at me out their car windows as we passed. Very friendly bunch. By that evening when I drove out to pick him up, even the large trucks were honking at me as they met me on the road. Hmmm, they are always friendly, but not quite this much.

By the time I was done making sausage and went back out to mine, almost every rig on the road was flashing lights and waving at me. I sent some of the sausage to work with Charlie to share at camp.

Just before Christmas, one of the men that had worked at the camp that summer stopped by our house in town. He asked if we had any of that sausage he could send to his elderly father for Christmas as his Dad had always wanted to try bear meat.

Charlie went down in the basement to check in the freezer for some and while he was gone, the man told me, "You know, when Charlie first told us that story, we all thought it was just another rumor getting started even though it was better than most." For once, I didn't spoil Charlie's stories and kept my mouth shut and just smiled. I didn't have a clue.

After the man left, Charlie looked at me and said he probably should explain what the man meant? Then he told me what he had done. We laughed a little and I started getting dinner. He looked at me a minute or two, then, "Just where did you get those bears?"

My worse scare with a human was the man that shoved the door open and knocked me down with a shove in my chest about 2 a.m. one night. I had a shotgun in my left hand and was raising and cocking it as he was reaching at me again. I don't know what he intended on doing, but I wasn't waiting to find out.

He did recognize the sound of the hammer going back, because he stepped back and started yelling at me to get out, they were moving in. That was the first time gold had reached almost $900 an ounce and they were planning on just moving in and working my claims. I told him to check with the State Division of Mining before he made more of a fool of himself. These were legal claims. There were 3 more men with the trucks and equipment in my yard, which is what had woke me to start with. A very good thing I was a fast dresser. He was still yelling that they would be back with the Troopers since I pulled a gun on them, I told him I would be right there. I never saw any of them again.

I spent about half of the summers by myself, mining. I am basically a lazy person, so worked out the easiest ways of doing everything. No job is too small to put off until tomorrow. The things that just can't be put off, are done with the least amount of effort. This way, I managed to raise a large garden, do the mining and still go gadding about.

I found myself living in much the same manner that my mother had, but without the hardship of it. I packed water, but used the pickup to do so. I raised and canned or cured a lot of our food, also because I wanted to. I butcher, can, cure and make sausage from bear, moose and caribou in season, because I like knowing what type of chemical is being added to my food. I do all these because I enjoy it.

I also have a generator, if I want electricity. I can take my laundry to town, if I want instead of hauling washing machine and generator to the stream. I don't HAVE to do any of this to survive. Quite a difference from earlier times.

Instead of walking through the brush marking out claim lines by hand, I paint one pad on the dozer track. Then I measured the distance for that line to come up again and figure how many times that painted pad must come up to equal one claim length. Then I sat on a nice soft seat, run the dozer around the claim and have the lines marked. See? Basically lazy.

There are three layers of carpet in the cabin now. Four in some high traffic areas. When the house or cabin get to be a health hazard, I'll sort things out a bit. Not too much, though. I kept house in town the same as at the cabin, I ignored it.

Charlie taught me a lot more than how to operate a dozer and a road grader. He also encouraged me to actually talk in front of other people. There were folks that had known me for years and never heard me speak. Probably thought I was mute. Now they wish I were. He was always my best friend, too.

A couple of years after I started spending summers at the mine, a fellow started a kennel for sled dog racing about a quarter mile down the hill from the cabin. By road, it was about a half mile. He kept pretty much to himself and worked very hard to establish his kennel and support his dogs. More dog mushers moved into the area and for the most part, were fairly compatible with gold mining. We used our roads and trails in the summer and they used them in the winter. They got a little testy when we moved one of our roads and started mining the area and what had been a trail became part of our dam.

We managed to keep things on an even keel and when the fellow below us married and started a family, his wife started doing a community pot luck once a month. It was very pleasant and we enjoyed it. She was an excellent cook and it was nice for both groups to get together socially. Most drank a bit and some smoked now and then. Since I did neither, I usually went home fairly early in the evening.

One night, everyone imbibed a bit freely and when one of the old time Miners and a lady musher fell asleep on the huge couch, the rest decided to pull a small prank on them.

They moved both people until they were side by side, then using a large needle and heavy thread, they sewed their clothes together. From the neck along the shoulder and down the arms, then on down the sides up the inseams and so on, both sets of clothing were firmly sewn in place.

Everyone sat around waiting, but the two victims slept on. Finally everyone wandered off, either to their own homes or to bed and asleep. Later, the lady woke up and attempted to brush her long hair away from her face, only to find her arm was very heavy and another hand smacked her face as she tried to rub. She got her eye open and found as she moved her arm, another arm moved with her.

She got her other eye open and discovered a sleeping face inches from her own. She tried picking threads loose, finally giving up and wriggling out of her clothes and then picking threads loose, glad that the elderly Miner was a sound sleeper. She redressed and went home.

A couple of years later, she was trying to attract sponsors and the old Miner happened to be at her place when the representative arrived. She was nervous and the old Miner jumped in to ease the tension by telling the guy about their getting sewn together as by that time he had heard the story many times. She wanted to punch him.

She was trying to impress the man as being a good family oriented icon to represent their products. They did go ahead and sponsor her, in spite of the story.

Charlie really enjoyed the Grandkids. The first time my daughter woke up and her baby was missing, she freaked out only to find that Charlie had taken him, after changing and dressing him for the "men" to have morning coffee over town. The fact that one of the "men" was only a couple of months old didn't matter. Men had to stick together. By the time he was 3 years old, they repaired things together and Kevin knew all the tools in the box. He would run and get whatever tool Charlie needed and brought the right one, the correct size, too.

When my daughter had moved from her basement bedroom to an apartment a few blocks away, Charlie missed them so much. She brought Kevin over often to work with his Grandpa.

Kevin with Charlie

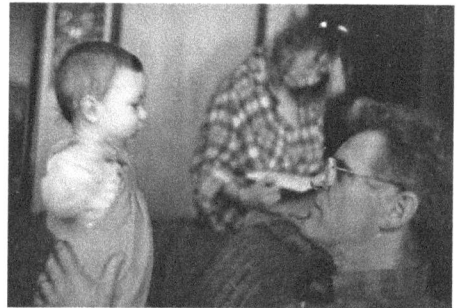
Samantha with Charlie

Paul & Kelsy with Charlie

Chapter 20

    Charlie asked my Mom what her wish would be, if she could have one thing in her life. She told him she would love to spend a summer out at the mine with me, painting and then drive back to Oregon, stopping wherever the mood struck.

    The summer of 1988, she came to Alaska early in the summer with her older sister and husband. They drove up the Alcan but she did not enjoy it as they did not stop to take pictures or look at the wild animals along the way.

    After they left, one of her younger brothers that used to come up almost every year arrived and they stayed in the old trailer house we had placed in a lovely area near the cabin. Neither one paid any attention to clocks, if they woke up and it was daylight, they got up and came to the cabin for a meal.

    Well of course it was daylight. This was summer in Interior Alaska and it is daylight all the time. After about a week of only a couple of hours sleep a night, then getting woke up with them wanting a meal, I set up cooking facilities in the trailer. I still prepared the evening meals, but they could fend for themselves the rest of the time. I didn't even mind making lemon meringue pies at 10 p.m., but once I finally got to sleep, I really like getting to stay there a few more hours than they did.

Mom and I painted every day, all summer. We set up the little improved bug free back room of the cabin as a studio and after doing my small amount of mining for the day, we painted. She soon picked up painting scenery quite well. We had a very good time.

Charlie put in an application for an early retirement application before we stopped mining for the summer, sometime in August. That's right, he had to apply for an application.

After closing up the mine for the winter and moving back to town, Mom and I packed the pickup and headed south. The trip as far as Whitehorse was fairly fast. There aren't too many diversions along the way. We did stop and take pictures when she wanted to.

The next night, we stayed at Tetsa River Lodge with people she had met on the trip north. We all got along very well and decided to spend a couple of days there, helping the lady out as her Mom hadn't arrived yet and a large shipment of groceries were delivered a week early. We helped her slice, dice and dehydrate a lot of the vegetables.

One night, as we were falling asleep in one of the small cabins, flickering light on the wall registered and I looked out the window to see flames leaping up from the smudge pot on the porch into the porch roof of another cabin across the yard.

I ran out the door barefoot and one toe went one way, the rest went the other around a stub on the ground. I was yelling before, trying to rouse Lori or the wrangler. The wrangler slept in the cabin between ours and the one with flames shooting into the eaves. After the toe thing, I was shrieking in pain, but still running over to the flames. Since my foot already hurt like the dickens, I kicked the smudge pot off the porch with my bare toes. Yeah, not too smart but I couldn't figure any way to get it off the porch before the building caught.

The wrangler stepped out his door in time to see the smudge pot roll under his lovely old vintage Cadillac. He got it started and backed off the pot before anything flared up under it. He hesitantly approached me and Mom was coming over by then, also as she had taken time to put on shoes. I explained to the wrangler and he shined his flashlight up under the eaves which were smoking and smoldering a bit. He got a fire extinguisher and dowsed that. We closed the tarp hanging over the unfinished doorway of the cabin that almost burned. They were using it to hang client's game animals in and were trying the smudge pot to keep flies out.

Late the next afternoon, Lori's husband rode in with his hunt clients and she didn't have anything ready for them. They weren't due for several more days. I offered to go cut a backstrap off an elk hanging in that cabin and she wasn't sure but let me go.

When I cut off a backstrap, I start up the neck as far as possible and go clear down to the hipbone on the rump. Then I coiled this long strip of meat around my arm and went back to her kitchen. I guess she had never seen a backstrap like that, before, she expected just the little short piece over the saddle.

Mom and I started slicing and pounding out the steaks to make chicken fried steaks and cream gravy. We ended up making two huge platters of steaks and about a gallon of gravy to go with the mashed potatoes, corn on the cob and green salad. I popped a fudge pudding cake in the oven while we ate dinner. Everyone was stuffed until it came out of the oven and we served it up with a scoop of vanilla ice cream on it with the hot fudge sauce over.

It was fairly late when we were going through the winter ski area north of Prince George. A black luxury car pulled up beside us and the driver rolled the passenger window down and pointed at my front wheel and motioned me to pull over to the side of the road.

I checked steering and nothing seemed wrong so kept on driving. The driver swerved his car over like he was going to nudge my pickup. I was driving a 1 ton 4 wheel drive crewcab pickup. Mom started sketching the car and we tried to make out the license plate. The entire car was spotless, but the license was smudged with dirt and not able to make it out. Mom sketched as much as we could see and shaded in a bit on it.

The driver pulled back in behind us and kept trying to get us to pull over. I finally pulled the little pellet pistol that was still in the tools on the driver's door of the pickup out and when the driver again swerved over toward us, I allowed the man to see that I did have a handgun and if he didn't leave us alone, I might even use it. The black car sped off down the road.

We pulled in to the first motel we came to with a vacancy. As the lady walked me over to our unit, I told her what had occurred, leaving out the handgun part. She got all excited. There were no official bulletins out, but lady tourists were disappearing in the area and they did not know how it was being done. We gave her Mom's sketches and she went in to call it in. I don't know what ever happened about that, but maybe they got it stopped.

We ended up going through Jasper Park which is gorgeous. The sheep along the road licked Mom's hand in the open window while we were taking pictures. At Lake Louise, the weather was getting very nasty so instead of staying the night there, we kept going and the road closed in behind us. We stopped at the Hot Springs and when we got around the next morning, the snow was visible just a little ways up the highway from our motel.

We crossed the Border into Montana near Whitefish and stopped for lunch there. Then we drove on to Glacier Park. My pickup was just barely legal to drive up the highway picked out by CCC workers during the Depression.

The views were staggering and the wild animals were lovely. I much prefer driving up that road to trying to drive back down it, so we circled around and got back on our way toward Oregon on a more southern route.

We had crossed the Rockies 5 times so far on our trip to Oregon. Not exactly the most direct way there. We would have checked out Yellowstone but it was on fire at the time. We couldn't even visit the Tetons because of the fires.

We traveled through the Sawtooth Mountains in Idaho and the weather was back to being very hot. This being an Alaskan pickup, air conditioning was not even something thought of as an accessory on it.

We used spray bottles of water with some mint added as coolers. We stayed saturated with the windows down for the air moving over us as much as possible.

We stayed with the lady in Boise, Idaho that I dragged to her plane just before getting caught with a gun in the airport a few years before. It was nice to see her again.

As soon as we crossed the Border into Oregon, we stopped and I bought a hunting license as they have to be bought before the start of the season a person wants to hunt in. Deer season was due to start in a couple of days. We stopped at a bean warehouse in Ontario and bought some 100 pound bags of beans and headed for the coast.

We crossed the high desert between Burns and Bend, then the Cascade Mountains and on to Eugene, over Route F to get Mom's pickup at her sister's house. We visited a while, then on to Siletz. It was really good to get there and not have to get up and drive the next morning so early although we planned on going back to Eastern Oregon to hunt for deer.

Mom's sister that lived in Toledo was going with us, driving her own pickup. She had an obnoxious little toy Doberman that bit everyone including her and yapped at everything. We might have gotten deer if that dog had stayed home or in the truck left at camp. We did have a lovely time camping up in the mountains on the back of a friend of theirs ranch.

Then we moved over to the Sisters area and set up camp up in the edge of one of the Three Sisters Mountains. That brought back memories.

It was beautiful but we never saw much game up there. We did enjoy the camping though and had a lovely camp set up.

After we got home to Mom's place, Charlie called and said he would fly down and drive back with me so I wouldn't have to make the trip by myself. I would go to Portland and pick him up at the airport there. I did it, but that big pickup wasn't easy to maneuver in heavy traffic.

We stopped in to see Archie on our way back to Mom's place from Portland. He was not doing well and it was so sad to see him like that. The family friend he was staying with was taking good care of him, but he was going downhill fast. We were very somber after leaving there.

Charlie framed in a greenhouse attached to Mom's house for her while we were at her place. We drove around and visited family along the coast. Finally it was time to head back for Alaska.

We loaded up the pickup and headed North by way of Eastern Oregon, yet again. We stopped at my sister's place and went to see Dad. My sister had to leave and help pack out an elk so we didn't stay very long. Daddy and Charlie got along well and Daddy was telling us great stories about some hunting he had done over the years.

We spent a very good time with him and I was sorry we had to leave so soon, but we had a freezer with no motor full of beef in the back of the truck and the weather here was warm with no dry ice available until we got to Walla Walla. We spent the night in Walla Walla and then on to Spokane.

Youngest stepson was living there at the time. As we knocked on the front door, he was escaping out the back window until he realized who it was. Maybe his choices hadn't improved all that much. We went out to lunch and visited with him a while, then he had to get to work, so we headed on north again.

We hit snow around Williams Lake in British Columbia. Then it was snow the rest of the way home.

When we stopped at Tetsa River Lodge, it was minus 22 degrees F. We stayed in the cabin the wrangler had used earlier as it had a heater. Charlie and Lori's husband Cliff really hit it off and visited for hours. We all really enjoyed that evening, but we couldn't turn off our pickup as it was diesel and at those temperatures, it wouldn't start again as they only ran their generator while they were awake and it wasn't large enough to handle the heaters on the pickup. So bright and early the next morning, we headed north yet again.

Whitehorse, Yukon Territory, was cold also, so we didn't dawdle long there, only catching a few hours' sleep and heading on for home.

It was wonderful to pull in our back alleyway and stop at our own house. We were home in time to have Thanksgiving dinner in a few days. We were super tired, but had to unload all the canned goods in the backseat of the truck so nothing would freeze and break. We got it unloaded and headed for bed.

The next morning, Charlie got called by the Union to go to work down at Clear Air Force Base the other side of Nenana. He passed the physical with flying colors. It was a four day on, three day off job and he liked it.

Charlie decided to continue trying for early retirement as he could still go back to work any time he wanted to and new jobs would still pay into his retirement so when he went back on it after a job was over, it would pay more per month. Not a bad deal. He had put in the application for the application way back in August and we had not heard anything from them yet. Finally, the day before Christmas the application came in the mail.

We had a very nice Christmas. Most of the kids were not at home, but every one called and talked for ages. The oldest stepdaughter and her kids came by to visit a couple of days before Christmas and it seemed Christmas lasted several days. My daughter was there with her three kids. The youngest of hers was only 4 months old and he was a big hit with the other kids as he was being very good. Of course everyone was holding him and telling him how cute he was, so why not?

    As we prepared for bed, Charlie hugged me and told me he loved me and I was the best part of his life. He did this once in a while and it always made me feel special to him. He certainly was for me.

Charlie

Charlie, my Grandmother, me, my Dad's older brother that lost a lung in WW I. Oregon.

PART FOUR - DISASTER

Chapter 21

"Goodbye, Sweetheart, drive carefully," I murmured drowsily as Charlie started down the stairs. It was 4:15 a.m., December 28, 1988 and Charlie is on his way to work at Clear Air Force Base, 80 miles from Fairbanks. The alarm had rang at 4:00 a.m. after a very short nights' sleep. Charlie would have plenty of time as his shift started at 8 a.m. but there is always the possibility of a flat tire.

We had time for our usual morning cuddle and kiss, very brief because of time, he dressed, went out and started the pickup, came back in for his small bag of clothes and a bag of groceries.

At this time of day he didn't feel like a cup of coffee or breakfast, so I didn't get up, we just talked as he got ready to leave. Usually we talked about the things needing done while he was at work during the week. Most weeks he would be gone 4 days, this being a holiday week, he only had three days before he would be home again.

The food at the mess hall at Clear left a lot to be desired so Charlie usually took groceries to have in his room. As soon as I heard the pickup back out of the drive, I started to doze back off to sleep.

"ROSE!" Charlie is calling me to get up, no, wait, Charlie left for work and I don't hear the truck. I must be dreaming. I should follow him down to Clear and surprise him at lunch. He would enjoy that. I'll just sleep a little longer so I don't get there too early and have to wait in the car.

The phone ringing at 8:10 a.m. woke me and with dread I heard Charlie's friend at work ask me if Charlie had overslept.

"No, he left at his usual time. Maybe he had a flat somewhere along the road or truck problems."

"We will start out from this end and see if we can find him," his friend said.

I was still half asleep but couldn't shake the feeling of foreboding. Charlie always had plenty of time for flat tires or minor mechanical problems. Why hadn't I asked Tom if there was something I could do?

This pacing around the house is driving me crazy. If I leave, Tom might call and say Charlie has shown up. If I stay here, I'll start climbing the walls. I decide to take a shower and leave the doors open so I can hear the phone. If I don't hear it, the answering machine will pick up the message. They will certainly call and tell me that Charlie is there any minute now.

It's 8:45 a.m. when Tom calls to let me know they are calling in the Troopers and start the search along the highway from both ends. I do remember to ask if there is anything I can do from this end and the answer is a resounding, "No."

The phone rings a little after 9 a.m., it's the State Troopers. They are willing to start flying the route, even though it won't be daylight for almost an hour yet. I'm not the only one worried, but I am the one that loves him. Why isn't there something I can do? Oh my Love, what has happened? Where are you?

A little after 10 a.m., I hear someone coming up the steps on the porch. It's an unfamiliar step and slow. A firm knock on the door almost as I swing it open. A lady city police officer was standing there and I feel like my world is coming to an end.

I invite her in and she starts telling me there has been an accident, here in town. How can that be? Charlie left hours ago. Maybe it's one of the kids. Are they all right? But no, she says it's my husband, my Darling, my Love. Is he injured or ill? No, she is saying, he didn't survive.

An accident? He was killed in an accident? I asked him to drive carefully. My mind is going numb, I can't believe this. No, she is saying, we believe he had a heart attack. There will have to be an autopsy, of course, since a death and a vehicle were both involved. But where did this happen? My mind is screaming but the words come out small, like a child.

Only 4 blocks from our house? He died only 4 blocks from home? When was he found? Only a little while ago? You mean he has been there all this time? No one noticed?

The fellows at Clear and the State Troopers are searching for him along the highway. She calls this information in to call off the search. She is being so kind and trying to get the necessary information from me, without upsetting me any more than I already am.

The facts, ma'am, nothing but the facts, from some old stupid show goes through my mind. Fact, he only got 4 blocks from home. Fact, he was feeling fine when he left here. Fact, he has been there almost 5 hours without anyone noticing anything. Fact, the truck knocked over a row of mailboxes and a street light and came to a stop in someone's driveway. But the only Fact, as far as my mind is concerned at this moment is, Charlie is dead and no one even noticed? How can this be? My whole world just tilted out of control and no one noticed?

My mind continues screaming while I try to act sane for this very gentle polite lady officer that has to do her job. She is very sweet and genuinely concerned for me. The edges of insanity must be peeping through at her as I try to push it back until she leaves. She stays. She tries to help prepare me for the things I will have to do in the next several days. People have to be notified. Charlie's wishes have to be fulfilled as to the final arrangements for disposal of the body. He had always been very precise as to what I was to do in the event of his death. Well, my Love, this is the last thing that I will ever be able to do for you, but I will follow your wishes to the best of my ability.

Finally, finally I am alone. I can rant and rave, scream and rage. Actually, I only cry. I cry and then as it seems to stop, I cry some more. It seems the tears will never stop. This, from a person that never cries. Oh my Darling, my Love, how can this terrible thing be? We were making so many plans, you were feeling so good, I love you so much. Never to see you again. I think the insanity is winning, surely I can take no more.

But I find that just because I don't want to deal with this doesn't mean it will go away. I call my daughter that lives a few houses away and calmly ask her to come over as soon as she can find a babysitter. I call our oldest daughter that lives a few miles from here and she has already left for work. I leave word with her husband. I call our son and daughter that live in Anchorage. No one home at either place, so I leave a message to call me as soon as possible.

I call Charlie's older brother in New York. He wants to know about funeral arrangements. Charlie didn't want a funeral. He wants to know about Services, Charlie didn't want any. Charlie wanted to be cremated, then his ashes spread to the four winds from a high hill out near our mining where we were so happy. This was his home, this is where he wants to stay.

He certainly did not want his remains to be shipped back to New York, the place he left the day of his last exam in high school and headed to Alaska, not even waiting for graduation. He finally picked up his diploma in 1975, they refused to mail it to him or allow his Mother to pick it up.

I call the mortuary. It's not as difficult to talk to the mortician as I thought it would be. He is very calm and matter-of-fact and I can deal with that. It's sympathy that undoes me.

I call my Mother, she is at work so I tell my brother that lives there with her. There is no phone to reach youngest son in Spokane, Washington. The police will try to notify him, but knowing him, he will be going out the back window. Old reflexes die hard.

My daughter is walking up the walkway and I dread having to tell her. Even though Charlie wasn't her biological father, she loves him dearly.

It's not any easier to tell her than I thought it would be. I don't have any idea how a person should do this, I've never dealt with the death of a Dearly Beloved. I don't know how anyone could prepare for it. I am so tired, I don't know how I will manage to stay awake and it is still early afternoon.

The phone rings, I answer. I seem to be on autopilot. The jobs needing done, are. My daughter has a bowl of soup with me for dinner, then has to go home to be with her three children. The night stretches before me. I have been alone many nights, I would have been alone tonight, in any case. Charlie would have been staying at Clear until the end of his work week. But now it seems different. Now I know he will never be coming home at the end of the week.

Oldest daughter called after getting home from work. I finally reach middle daughter after she got home. Oldest son returned my call after a day of skiing. Now, only the youngest son is unaware he is a semi-orphan. In Anchorage, Doug went over to be with his sister and her young son so at least they will be together. Tonight will not be easy for any of us.

My Mother called as soon as she got home from work and we cried to each other on the phone for half an hour before we could speak.

The afternoon newspaper has a large photo of our truck, the caption reads, "Morning Accident – Fairbanks City Police are investigating an accident in which an elderly man was found dead in this pickup truck after it left the road and crashed through a light pole in the 100 block of Farewell Avenue at about 9 a.m. today. Next of kin had not been notified by press time."

Not very much of that was accurate. Charlie was only 60 years old. That is not elderly. He died around 4:30 a.m. at the latest, not 9 a.m., so much for the accuracy of the press. Is this really only Day One?

It is impossible to sleep. I doze in fits and starts, always awakening in tears. Will they ever stop? My eyes feel gritty and dry, yet the tears flow.

After several hours, I get up. I search through photos to find a good photo of Charlie for the paper. I don't know why, but the caption for their photo last night really irked me. Charlie and elderly did not fit in the same sentence. He was vibrant and alive, a wonderful lover and friend. None of those things fit the description of 'elderly'. As soon as the newspaper office opens, I call. I give the correct information to the obit editor and will drop off the picture on my way to the mortuary.

Some of my daughter's friends have offered to care for her children for a few days so she comes over to stay with me. I am not sure of driving by myself in my present mental state and am glad of her company. She is one of the few people that seems to realize they do not have to be talking or entertaining me all the time. The tears will start at unexpected times, but so do hers so I am not so self-conscious about it.

We stop at the newspaper office, then drive several miles to the mortuary. The paperwork is simple and straightforward. The Mortician is very good at his job and keeps us at ease while discussing terrible things.

After leaving the Mortuary, we go over to file the paperwork for the coming year of mining. Charlie and I had decided on the coming year's layout and I was supposed to have filed these papers yesterday. I will still have to mine to make a living somehow.

Everyone at the Division of Mining know about Charlie and everyone wants to hug me and sympathize. I can't handle this. These are our friends, but I just can't. How does a widow deal with a funeral and services? I can't even deal with random well-wishers.

We do get the papers filed and they even fill out and send the Federal Agency papers that need to be dealt with.

I have to thank Charlie for his decision on early retirement. He got his paperwork and had it notarized and mailed off day before yesterday. I would at least have his pension, thanks to his foresight.

We finally make it home. It feels like we have gone through a major day's work and it is not even noon. I feel exhausted, my cheeks are wet and I don't even realize I am crying again. The light is rapidly blinking on the answering machine, I write down the messages but can't handle calling back at this time. Maybe later.

Today's paper is out shortly after 1 p.m. and the phone starts ringing within minutes and it seems to ring ever few minutes the rest of the day and evening. Everyone is stunned by Charlie's death. I am wiped out by it. I am getting paranoid. What do these people want from me? Am I just satisfying their morbid curiosity in details? Why are they asking for all the details? Why don't they just leave me alone? I can certainly understand "I just want to be alone," much better now.

I know these people aren't ghouls, they just want to express their shock, sorrow and sympathy, but it doesn't make me feel any better. Maybe I will appreciate this all at a later date when I think back on it all. This evening, I just feel like a zombie, going through the motions, devoid of emotion or feeling. Emotions and feelings hurt and I just can't take any more hurt at this time.

My daughter is asleep on the couch so I go to bed. She is sleeping away her grief and I can't seem to sleep at all. I wish I could. This is Day Two.

I cuddle a giant stuffed toy and revert to childhood but it doesn't make me sleep. My eyes are scratchy and dry, my throat is raw and at any other time, I would think I was coming down with flu or a very nasty cold. I have wiped my nose so much, my upper lip is raw and sore. Certainly not anyone's idea of the beautiful widow. Oh well, I wasn't beautiful before, either. Before and After? It feels like a giant knife has sliced off my life. I know it will never be the same, After.

Day Three is almost a repeat of Day Two's afternoon and evening. The phone replaces human contact. I am notified by the Coroners' Office that Charlie definitely had a massive heart attack and was dead before impact of the vehicle. At least my Love didn't have to suffer a long illness or ravaging disease. He would have hated that. This is the way he would have wanted to go but I wanted at least 20 to 30 more years of his loving company.

It's not fair. I know life doesn't have to be fair, but it's still so not fair. There are so many totally worthless excuses of humanity wandering around out there, still alive and Charlie is dead.

I really have to keep a rein on myself because I find I want to personally correct this situation. If I am in the car, I want to swerve over and send them on their way. This can not be normal. The craziness is trying to break free and I can't allow that. It peeps through at terrible times and is scary.

Charlie operated the lead dozer while building the Haul Road over Atigun Pass. It was built from the top down. That small dot on the cut is a D-9 dozer he was running.

Looking down from the cut. Atigun Pass.

Chapter 22

The mortuary calls, I can pick up Charlie's ashes on Tuesday since Monday is a holiday. I need to bring copies of Charlie's military discharge papers with me. Veterans get a Death Benefit from the Government. That is such a contradiction of terms, Death Benefit. What is the benefit of being dead? Dead is dead, there is no benefit in that.

I write letters to inform some of the family and friends that I didn't notify by phone. I photocopy the newspaper pictures and notices to include in the letters. I don't know an easy way to tell people. It seems so cold to say Charlie died, but I can hardly write a chatty letter, then add at the end of it – Oh, by the way, Charlie died. How does one do these things? Still the tears fall, is there an endless source of them? I never realized a person was capable of so many tears.

My daughter awakens after a solid 12 hours of sleep. I envy her the ability to sleep. It seems like forever since I have slept. I am so tired I can barely function, yet I can't sleep. The two kids living in

Anchorage will be up here this weekend. She will drive up with her son, he will fly up that evening.

My daughter has gone home to check on her children and change her clothes. Oldest daughter stopped by. I told her I turned in the paperwork on her pickup at the same time I did mine as they were both through the same company and Charlie had signed on both of them. I should have waited a couple of months and then told her.

Middle daughter got here from Anchorage with her 7 year old son on the evening of Day Three. She is taking this about the same way I am, poor girl. She probably should not have driven all that way with just her young son for company. Her son is bewildered but then, so am I. I feel so inadequate to deal with this.

So much sorrow on top of our years of joy. I'll have to keep remembering the joy, but that makes me angrier about not having even more years with him. Oldest son gets in later that night. I'm worried because his plane is late. I seem to worry about everyone now. Will the roads be dry? Will there be too much snow? Will there be ice? Will the plane arrive safely? This is nerve wracking. It is good to see everyone but not under these circumstances.

Tom from Charlie's work at Clear stops by. The fellows he worked with took up a collection of cash to help me out with immediate expenses. They also brought me a bouquet of flowers. They said they realized Charlie didn't want flowers but maybe they would make me feel better. How sweet of them to do this.

Day Four is here. I guess they will keep doing this to me, the rest of my life. One day after the next. The kids go back to Anchorage. There really isn't much that can be done except reaffirming our love for each other. I gave the oldest son the rifle Charlie wanted him to have. It used to belong to his Great-grandfather. I gave him his Grandfather's silver watch, also. I gave his sister the silverware her Grandmother had given me. I think these are things they should have from their family's past.

I also gave him the Apple II+ computer. I have had it almost a year and am still not comfortable working on it. All I really need is a word processor that doesn't require any more thought than a typewriter to work. I'm not even a good typist, I am certainly not a computer buff.

Now I will worry about their trip home until I hear from them. This is ridiculous, they are grown adults and capable of caring for themselves and have been for some years now. My worrying will not help nor do any good.

What a depressing New Year's Eve this is. Charlie and I had planned to finish drinking the bottle of sparkling cider in a toast, tonight, then watch the fireworks. We drank the first half on Christmas Eve and toasted our future. I pour the rest of the bottle down the drain. It certainly did not do much for our toast together.

My daughter is asleep on the couch, she can hardly stay awake. I sit here, watching the fireworks by myself. Usually the fireworks are spectacular with all the snow. Tonight, everything is dull. The clouds are low and light snow is drifting down. A fitting night for my present mood. She had wanted to watch the fireworks but I can't rouse her. She mumbles and grouses then falls back asleep. I think it is the best thing she can do. I just wish I could, too.

New Years Eve, this is supposed to be a night of renewal, a night to make resolutions, a night to carouse with friends and loved ones. My loved one is now represented by a pile of ashes in a mortuary. My resolution is, I will survive. Thus endeth Day Four.

Sunday, Day Five. I get a call from Anchorage, they made it home okay. My daughter is groggy from too much sleep and feeling guilty because she sleeps and I can't. I guess each body deals with grief in its' own way. I just wish mine would allow sleep. I feel decidedly punch drunk. The phone is quiet for longer periods of time. I don't think I could handle too many more calls like a couple I have gotten. Some people seem to feel I should have visitation and services, regardless of what Charlie wishes.

All I can think of is one funeral we attended of a friend and Charlie saying, "Please, please don't ever do that to me." I can not bring myself to do something so entirely against his wishes. If people wanted to show him how much they liked and respected him, it should have been done while he was alive to appreciate it, not as a sop to their conscience after his death.

I know some people tend to idealize the person that has died. I don't think I will do that. He was a wonderful person and he was dearly loved and respected in life. He was also stubborn at times and opinionated at other times. We had definite differences of opinion on many things in our life together but that did not detract from the love and respect. He was an intelligent, capable and loving individual and oh, how I miss him.

Monday, Day Six. A holiday, so there is not much I can get done today. We sit around and mope all day. Not very good for either of us.

We finally ran out of the big pot of soup I had made for Charlie and I for our last evening together. I would certainly have made something special had I but known. It was a meal he liked, split pea soup with lots of ham and vegetables, served with hot biscuits. Oh Love, all the what if's and if onlys that go through my mind. Does everyone go through these feelings after the loss of a loved one? Am I truly unhinged? Insane seems inappropriate but unhinged sounds the way I feel. Something that once was together but is now dangling, mostly in mid-air.

Tuesday, Day Seven. Today there are many things I must do. First, I must call the garage to arrange towing of the truck from police impound. Then contact impound to make sure someone is there. The tow truck driver came by and gave me a lift to the impound lot. As registered owner, I am the only one that can sign the release of the truck. I sign, then we go out to the truck. It looks far worse than the picture in the paper led me to believe. The whole front end is caved in, the windshield is smashed and the entire passenger side is crumpled in. The truck certainly looks terrible. It's a 1 ton 4x4 crewcab Ford diesel, only one and a half years old.

All of the tools are still in the back in the big box across the bed of the truck. All the groceries are frozen in the front seat. Charlie's bag of personal belongings is still here. The police had told me they would take everything out of the truck at the scene of the accident and that I would have to pick them up from the Coroners' Office. The doors of the truck were even still unlocked, all 4 of them. The bag looks like it has been searched thoroughly and sloppily. I wonder if all his things are still in it?

The tow truck driver has a hard time using his little tow truck to haul this large pickup. We finally make it out of the impound lot and he takes me home. He helps me unload all the stuff from the pickup including the big tool box. He is being very kind to me and I appreciate it.

Kara and I go over to the Coroners' Office and pick up Charlie's personal belongings. All the photos he had in his wallet are missing. They do not return his clothes or his heavy winter coat that would have been on the seat beside him while driving. Any cash will be returned to the estate in about a month. I ask for a copy of the Coroner's report, she says it will be ready in about a month, also.

After we leave the Coroner's Office, we go out of town to the Mortuary and pick up Charlie's ashes. As depressing days go, this one is a dilly. I have a piece of paper that needs to be signed and returned to the mortuary after disposition of ashes. I don't want to be doing this. I want to go home, sleep, awaken and find that this is all a horrible nightmare. This time my nightmare has become the reality. Maybe this is why I can't sleep. I am asleep. Please, someone, anyone, wake me up.

So goes Day Seven. I hope to never have another one as bad. Even in the presence of death, Life continues whether we want it to or not. So many things have to be taken care of. In private, I wallow in grief. I absolutely give myself over to misery, crying until my eyes are swollen almost shut and my face is puffy beyond recognition. By allowing myself to do this in private, I seem to hold it together better in public.

Around midnight, my daughter had to be rushed to emergency. They gave her pain killers and schedule an ultrasound. Later, we find that she had several large gallstones and after a routine Pap smear, there is a possibility of cervical cancer. She is only 24 years old. Will this ever stop?

She has gotten a tiny black kitten for me, the runt of the litter and very small and cute. Charlie thought they were darling, a couple of weeks ago but they were still too young to leave their mother at that time. He always said he didn't like cats, but always loved ours just as much as I did. I guess it is a lot like children, I don't care for most other peoples', but love my own dearly.

Jack, the fellow that stays in the spare room in our basement between jobs arrives about midnight the next night. He only stays until he gets another job. This time he is returning from a family visit in New York and brought back a frozen quarter of venison. That has to be taken care of immediately, so I trim, cut and can most of it. That keeps me busy a few hours.

Now I have two kittens. The little female seemed lonesome and the person that was going to take the male reneged. She really doesn't appreciate the thoughtfulness. She might have been lonely, but she was getting to like being only cat. She is only half his size, but has already chewed all the hair off the back of his ears and beats him up every time he gets near her. Poor little fellow. I have tentatively named them Beauty and Beast, but she is the one acting beastly.

Walking through the grocery store I see the card display and start to cry before I even realize it. I always picked out special and sometimes funny cards for Charlie and put them in his bag to find at work. If he was up North working, I sent them in the mail.

It's a good thing I am not a helpless sort of female. The furnace quit at 32 degrees below zero F. last night. Jack is still here but knows nothing about furnaces. I have it running again before he realizes it was down. I took a short course in boiler operation a few years ago and am licensed by the State of Alaska as a boiler operator. The furnace is an oil fired hot water boiler.

What do women do that have never handled any of these things do? I have always repaired whatever needed repairing or ran equipment when we mined. A few days ago, I plowed the snow from our driveways with our small dozer.

These are things expected of me, since Charlie usually worked up North during the winter. Minor repairs and maintenance are really not that difficult, it is just intimidating to some to start. It is also best to give it a try when there is no one else around to make you feel inadequate while you figure it out. Charlie never did that, but lots of people do.

The Union is trying to get out of paying me the pension the way Charlie set it up. They want to only give me half the amount each month. They offer me more than double that amount if I agree to only receive it for 5 years, then nothing.

I would not be able to continue living in this house if things go their way. They are saying Charlie had to be alive and receive at least one check before death to activate the 100% spouse option. I asked to see a copy of that from their by-laws or regulations as no one in the local office had ever heard of such a thing. So far, the Union's Life Insurance hasn't paid off either. I think they are trying to make me desperate enough to accept their offers.

I finally mention that if they had sent the application out right after he asked for it, he would have received a couple of months checks, anyway, and he did send it back in as soon as he got it. We'll see.

Charlie didn't have a Will. I don't know what the Court will do on disposition of property. Most of our stuff was owned jointly with Right of Survivorship, but the attorney is asking for copies of all the titles, including joint property. That doesn't seem necessary to me. There were only three items not jointly owned yet she is making a major case out of this. I think I should have talked to someone else first.

Grizzlies at the cabin.

Charlie with runway fish.

Chapter 23

I think I have figured all this mess out. There is a conspiracy to confuse, bewilder and anger the newly bereaved. This way, anger replaces grief as the main emotion felt. I know that is the way it is working for me. Even the weather is nasty.

We are in the midst of a record breaking cold spell. It lasted about six weeks and seldom got up to minus 40 degrees F. and hitting in the minus 50 and minus 60 degree F. range. It even made national news.

The intersections around town are littered with "Alaskan snakes", broken fan belts from the cars running in such cold weather. Then the light turns green, the driver accelerates and pop, another Alaskan snake joins its flock.

Just the business of survival becomes most important. My daughter's middle child had her second birthday during this. I baked a cake, Jack bought some ice cream and we took it over for a mini-birthday party.

It's over a month now and I still don't want anyone to touch me. I flinch when well-wishers want to hug me and feel nauseous. I don't even want anyone to be very close to me without touching. This is a terrible feeling and I hope it goes away. I've never liked to be casually hugged, my knee tends to automatically come up, but this is way beyond that feeling. It's carrying anti-social behavior to a bit of an extreme.

I just received a letter from the Union office in Seattle. I think it means they are going to honor the option Charlie chose for the pension. I won't believe it until I see the checks start arriving. The power company and utilities companies are threatening disconnection as I have no money at all and am living off the food in the house.

What a terrible awakening this morning. It was my terrible nightmare all over again. The phone rang at quarter after 7 a.m. The voice said it was Clear Air Force Base and was Wes oversleeping this morning? Wes? That was the only thing different, but in my sleep clogged brain, it took a while for the wrong name to soak in.

What finally did soak in was, someone else is missing from work at Clear. His name must have been beside Charlie's and the fellow dialed our number by mistake. What a horrible sense of déjà vu. That really got my day off to a miserable start.

Then tomorrow is Charlie's birthday. Not a great weekend, emotion-wise.

My sister called. Our Father is in the hospital, nothing serious, she said. He is 87 years old and just about anything can be serious at that age so she took him for peace of mind. Good girl.

Three months have passed, now. I still have sudden crying spells for no apparent reason. They are fewer and farther between. Most of the gastro-intestinal disorders have calmed down. I am able to eat at least once a day without nausea or diarrhea.

I have begun to feel sexual need again. That was a real surprise to me. I used to feel that any extended period without sex was a hardship, then to feel complete aversion for the last three months and now some feeling returning is confusing. I still don't want anyone to touch me and the thought vaguely nauseates me.

The Probate still drags on. All I needed was named Executor of the Estate. I know how to type up legal papers, I could have managed to do the quitclaim deeds needed for the mining claims and talked to the State about the Homesite Charlie had to see if it is possible to change over or not. How difficult would that be? I think they just enjoy getting the check each month that they are charging me for this simple thing.

I have made out a Will, specifying exactly who gets what. By the time I am dragged off stage kicking and screaming, I may not still own any of the present property, but everyone will know what I had in mind.

Jack has been evicted. He came over where I was working in the kitchen, put one arm around my shoulders, his head on my shoulder and the other hand on my boob, telling me he was so lonely. What the heck? Not happening, even if he wasn't already married.

Seekins Ford still isn't done with repairing the pickup. Three weeks ago they called and said it was done. When I looked at it, the huge dent in the roof from the light pole was still there, dark paint was spattered over the top and driver's side and bare metal showing along the side that was crunched. What a good place for repairs.

I have finally received the small life insurance and a pension payment from the Union. Now I am at least out of that section of limbo. Unless I get really crazy with the money or inflation hits big time, I won't lose the house Charlie built by himself.

I went ahead and filed for an extension on the Homesite we were working on. I can't finish the building in time by myself and don't want to lose it, either.

To work on the Homesite, which is 20 miles from town and part of that is on a road we built (very basic road) I bought a used Nissan pickup. That road needed 4 wheel drive most of the time and it is rough trying to haul supplies in the car. I am making progress, but it is very slow.

I still do everything as though Charlie were only at work up at Prudhoe Bay or Barrow or on the D.E.W. Line. Sometimes we would be separated for several months at a time while he worked. I guess it has probably helped my ability to cope with the day to day problems around the house and property. I still find myself crying at unfortunate times.

I have always worn lightly shaded glasses, now I have darker shading so the red eyes don't show so much. Nothing masks the puffy face and swollen nose.

I seem to go through life in a haze of unreality. I don't know whether it is the right thing to do or not, but at least I cope doing it this way. I still file things in my mind to tell Charlie when he gets home. Then I have to remind myself, no, he will never be coming home. I buy things to suit Charlie's tastes, whether it be clothing, food, or whatever, possibly more than I did when he was alive.

I put on the Trade Show for the Placer Mining Conference held in Fairbanks each Spring. That paid me enough to cover the property payments and ¾ of the year's insurances. It also requires a lot of time and energy. By forcing myself to get out and do all the things necessary for a successful Trade Show, I seem to have helped my mental self a bit. The Conference itself was rather nerve-wracking.

Many of the people were friends that Charlie worked with for years but were still unaware of his death. It's very hard to interrupt someone that is all jokes and happiness about Charlie not being there, is he off running around?

At least I don't just blurt out "Shut up, Charlie's dead." I use a bit more tact than that, but once in a while, not by much. I usually always made the sanctuary of a restroom before the tears got totally out of control. It was a very rough 5 days.

I find that by writing everything down, most as it was happening and updating it once in a while has helped me deal with my sorrow and grief. A friend gave me a book soon after Charlie died that suggested doing that and it was right. The book is titled "The Widow's Handbook, A Guide for Living,"

That book has been of much help to me. It helped me understand that a lot of the emotions and physical problems I was experiencing are normal to grief. It also spelled out things I would need to do that had never entered my mind. The book was written by Charlotte Foehner and Carol Cozart. Thank you Ladies, you helped me more than I can say.

I finally no longer feel cold all the time. No matter how many layers of clothing I put on or how high I turned the thermostat, I could not get warm. I would even half scald myself under the shower and within a matter of minutes I would feel as chilled as ever. I had a deep cold hollow feeling in my chest that just refused to leave.

I can not tell what day it finally disappeared, but now I realize that it has left. Will the other miserable feelings leave the same way? Silently, with no fanfare? I don't know.

Today is April 7, 1989. Today I was finally appointed by the Court to represent the Estate. I also received a copy of the Coroners' report. I have not the courage yet to open the report. She warned me that it would be very graphic. This is not something recommended for the survivors to do. If or when I do read the report, I will first assure total privacy for myself. Probably late some night. Maybe never. Possibly this will finally make my mind realize once and for all, Charlie is never coming back. He is not just away at work. I may never read that report.

By now you probably understand me well enough to know, I could never let something be. Yes, I read the report. It was almost a year later and it just reconfirmed what I had been told earlier. A massive heart attack and as instant as death can be. No suffering or lingering in pain. No advance notice evidently. Just minutes before, we had been talking and laughing together, making plans, kissing goodbye. Goodbye forever on this earth.

Several months after Charlie's death, I was feeling a return of desire for sex, but did not want anything to do with anyone on a more personal level. A recent acquaintance I met while checking out whether or not it would be simpler and cheaper to buy a log cabin shell to finish on the Homesite or try to finish building the small start we had made, and I talked it over in a dispassionate manner.

He never wanted a real relationship either so we decided to just be in it for a strictly physical relationship and nothing else. This worked quite well for several months.

We had been trading labor and knowledge on building projects, I did dozer work for him on his property and he helped on finishing the construction of the cabin on the Homesite (I didn't buy the cabin shell he was selling when I met him). I had been keeping an album of photos taken through all the stages of building that cabin, the road in to it and several calendars with the time spent living up there. I got the patent on the Homesite.

Then a friend was diagnosed with terminal cancer. She wanted to go to Greece for an alternative treatment and asked me to accompany her. We were gone almost a month and she went into remission. When we returned home, I found things had changed. I now had a roommate. He rented out his own home and was firmly moved into mine. He also decided he liked living with someone and wanted to get married. That totally blew it.

While we were still arguing things out, we went to Valdez to go fishing with a friend of his that owned a nice boat. We caught a few fish, but no halibut which is what I really wanted. We did get a couple of bears.

We hung them in my basement and the next day, I set up out in the yard to start cutting them up. A skinned out black bear looks very much like a human. I didn't have a large kitchen, so set up a sheet of plywood on 2 sawhorses out by the faucet from our well. There was also an electrical outlet by it, so I took my little electric chainsaw out to cut ribs into shortribs. Most of the meat would be made into sausage.

My daughter, her 3 young children and boyfriend were staying in the front apartment on the house and the night before, before I got home, they had a screaming noisy fight that everyone in the neighborhood must have heard. He stomped out but no one saw that part, then it was very quiet.

The next day, here I come, carrying a large skinned out body from the basement and plopped it on my makeshift work table and started dismembering it and throwing the pieces into the rinsed out wading pool the kids used.

The neighbor across the street kept her curtains twitching as she watched through the slit she held open. I am very surprised that no police showed up. Then I hauled out the larger body and dismembered it, also. The lady would run for her car if she came out of her house and I was in sight, after that.

Later, when food was disappearing from my freezer, I left some skinned out bear feet in plastic bags in there, with names on them of the clients they were to go to, after being cleaned. However, a front foot looks like a hand and a hind foot looks like a human foot. Once those were placed in sight in both freezers, I never lost any more food out of those freezers. I did the same, later, in Utah while doing some mounts for clients down there from our hunts. It probably helped that they were labeled with the men's names that the bones would go to, after they were cleaned.

Things went swiftly downhill with him. As that was dragging through its final phases; I was working on the mining with some nice men. One had been divorced for 8 years and was firmly anti- marriage.

He and I got along well working together and I started to have feelings I thought were gone forever. I even enjoyed having him hug me in greeting. Then things progressed beyond that point and I really enjoyed. I couldn't believe it, I fell in love. I didn't want to admit it to myself, let alone tell him, but I did. It is not an easy thing for me to do, this loving business. The physical stuff is easy.

I was Secretary of the Alaskan Independence Party for many years. Not that I actually have any secretarial skills, but I draw a mean cartoon so did make a lot of people not real happy. I successfully ran for defeat by nominating someone else for my job when it started to get popular to be in our Party. We even got a Governor elected. Working with Joe Vogler was always interesting.

I took 3 semesters at the University of Alaska, Fairbanks, in metal smithing and now can make jewelry and small sculptures with what gold I find.

Just as I was getting set up to start working at that on a more commercial scale, I had to sell all the gold we had saved, to pay Charlie's kids. The family's New York property had sold, the funds were for the heirs but the attorney for the estate told me the first check was made out to each surviving spouse for being the spouse of an heir. I believed him and used the money to replace the furnace. The kids said it was supposed to all be for them and threatened lawsuit, so I sold gold and repaid them. I'm not going to fight the kids. So I am pretty much out of that business for a while. Probably forever.

My first bull moose, 1989

Dipnetting at Chitina

PART FIVE – DUMBASS YEARS, REVISITED
Chapter 24

I started work as a Class A Assistant Guide for a friend starting a Guide business. Might as well put all my years of hunting to some other use besides just putting meat on the table. Every spring, we did the black bear hunts and in the autumn, it was grizzly and moose hunts. I passed my Registered Guide exam and got licensed. Now the Guide I worked for, could let me set up camp in a separate area without his having to come to camp at least once during each hunt. Easier for both of us.

I guess I can add this license to the Boiler Operator license, the Taxidermy License and the Sawmill Operator rating. Like I said before, anything to keep from doing housework.

I renewed my taxidermy skills from many years ago. I did some, while living in Wrangell, but the supplies were part of the items left behind during the move up here. So now my house had the addition of assorted animals in various stages of undress. Mostly bears from clients of our hunts.

We had a new client in camp one night, a retired psychologist that came out to hunt camp as much for the chance to tell his stories as to hunt. He was an avid hunter and traveled the world just to hunt. The man was an excellent shot and a black powder enthusiast. He had just been corresponding with a hunter in South Africa and swapping recipes for their loads and lead. He was anxious to try out some of the new lead on this trip.

Being the first night of a week-long hunt, he wanted to spend the evening just observing on a ground stand at one of the bait stations and take some video and just have a captive audience for the evening. The cook's helper was a girl from Eastern Oregon ranch country, also wanting to see some bears, so the 3 of us headed upriver to a nice station, where lots of immature bears had been using the station.

Nothing large had been spotted in the area and it would be okay to chat and photograph a lot of younger bears asserting dominance and arranging the pecking order.

The stand was a ground stand, a fallen log with some brush piled up around the front of it and chairs for client and guide to sit on in comfort with the river directly behind us. We had settled in and had one comedian of a bear that seemed to enjoy the attention, we had taken lots of photos and video, eaten most of the backpack of snack items and listened to many tales of hunting around the world, when the client decided to try out a cub call he had found somewhere in his travels. At first, it sounded horrible, but he finally got it down pat and was making lots of cries of a lost cub, nothing happened, so he decided to open a can of sardines.

As he bent down to rummage through the backpack, I saw a large furry back thrashing through the underbrush; about 2 feet higher than the 3 year old bear that had been entertaining us all evening. Afraid my moving might startle the bear, I kicked the client's shin to get his attention (the cook's assistant later asked me if I actually get paid to abuse the clients.) He responded very well, in slow motion he raised back to sitting position while bringing his rifle up in the same slow easy motion.

That bear was huge. He also was not slowing down for the bait station; he was barreling straight toward the last location of that lost cub. When it became obvious that bear was not slowing down, I agreed it was a good bear to shoot.

The client calmly shot and we all saw the fur fluff out at impact site. The bear whirled, biting at the opposite side, and running back the way he had come from. We just knew that was a really good solid hit and sat back to wait a few minutes to give the bear time to lay down and die. We tied a white flag to a stick on the riverbank, the signal to come pick us up.

The client went ahead and ate his sardines, cook's helper and I went over and cleaned up around the bait station and the blood sign where the bear had been hit, tied a piece of surveyors tape to a branch to mark the blood trail and then we set out to find the bear. The client had bad ankles from injuring them jumping off a bluff on a hunt earlier in the year. I had knee surgery a few months earlier and was still on a crutch and leg brace.

We just knew that bear couldn't have traveled far. However, at each large clump of brush or large stump or tree, that bear had doubled back and watched his back trail a bit, there would be 2 splashes of blood, one on each side where he had laid down and blood gushed out. We tied another piece of surveyors' ribbon.

Not being one of those dumb guides that lead a client that has lost an animal, I walked a couple of feet behind and to one side and the cook's helper did the same on the other side, each with our weapons ready.

About a mile later, after walking through thick brush and a small bog, so good on both of us crips, we were coming up a small rise when I saw a flicker of movement ahead, I placed my hand on the client's shoulder and some pressure back, he stepped back instead of forward just as the bear swung his paw around the base of the clump of brush, swiping right through where the client would have stepped. Client was good and got another shot off with his rifle, again we could see a perfect shot, into the fur on that bear, and again, that bear ran.

We stood and looked at each other a couple of moments then continued on, following the bear.

He got another shot as the bear went into the trees, and we were not sure on the placement of that shot, but this bear should have been dead quite a ways back. We finally caught up with the bear in a swale farther into the trees; the bear was down, but still attempting to swipe at us and snapping his teeth at us. The client was feeling terrible and asked me to finish the bear, since his rifle wasn't doing the job. I said no, and handed him my pistol and he did the final shot behind the ear.

We sent the cook's helper back to the river bank to flag down the boat that was supposed to pick us up; we had her hang a pair of red satin underpants on a limb over the river, since the white tie we had put out earlier didn't seem to get them to stop for us. Three other boats stopped to see if we wanted help, then. (The red panties were in the sleeve of my coat to keep people from claiming my coat in camp, it worked, I never lost another coat.)

The client and I started skinning and by the time we were finished, we were really puzzled. All 3 of his rifle shots had hit in the kill zone. All we could figure, was the loads that worked well in Africa must have been too hard and didn't mushroom at all, the exit holes were as small as the entrance holes, and no damage internally, except small holes right on through organs. The bear had finally almost totally bled out, but took quite a bit of time and a lot of distance. The guide I was working for at the time finally followed our surveyor tape trail and helped us carry out the hide, skull and better cuts of meat.

The client stayed on in camp for his week and we fleshed out the hide and salted it down well, and cleaned out the skull so we could take it to be sealed at Fish & Game in town. He gave me a good tip when he left camp.

He hired me to do the taxidermy work on it, later, after the tannery in town tanned the hide. The bear was a very large male, over 6 ft. 6 inches from nose to tail.

In Interior Alaska, we don't weigh bears, ours are long, lean and mean. They are in direct competition with the grizzlies and a grizzly loves to have a black bear for dinner. Certainly not the wussy bears they are in the Lower 48. Of course, in the Lower 48 all aggressive bears have been weeded out over a few hundred years so only the timid wussy bears get to procreate. It makes a difference in attitude.

When I was guiding down river on another hunt, one of the Assistants managed to slash his thigh with chainsaw kickback. It looked like a bear slashed his leg with 4 ragged slashes. The boat was not due back to check on us for another week.

We washed out the cuts as best we could with boiled water, then I handed him the bottle of betadine and made him pour it over his leg. After he quit jumping, cussing and swinging his fists around camp, we super glued his leg back together and butterfly bandaged with some duct tape strips. I checked his leg every evening and swabbed it a bit more with betadine, then covered with bag balm and he recovered very well with no infection. We were lucky.

I enjoyed working as a Guide. Most of our clients were very nice and knowledgeable outdoorsmen and women. There were only one or two over the years that I would have preferred to leave out there as bait. Since I did the taxidermy work for several of the clients, I kept in touch until the jobs were done. The Guide I worked for told me to keep in touch with all my clients as I would need letters of recommendation from them when I got my own license. He was right.

Only one has stiffed me on the job of preparing and making his charging bear wall mount. For the most part, I found hunters and fishermen to be a fine group of people.

One of the groups we had for one of the fishing trips wasn't so great. A father/son team that should have booked a room in a hotel with a good bar and they would have been fine. The son's mother-in-law died the night they arrived, but they didn't want to cancel and take a raincheck on the trip, so we proceeded. They brought expensive leather luggage (large) for a remote fly in fish camp with limited space.

The largest suitcase clanked of glass bottles and somehow it managed to get dropped several times on the rocks as we exited the small plane. Dragging it up the silt bank somehow it clanged against a few more obstacles so the vodka pouring out once it reached the top was not a surprise.

The father complained about everything, the son turned up the huge boombox he considered a necessity and they stayed in the cabin most of the time arguing and drinking. They had brought a tackle box full of lures that might have worked fine in some sort of fishery, but were not appropriate for pike which is what we were guiding for.

They would wake up late, argue a while, then decide to go fishing around 1 or 2 in the afternoon, so the other fish guide would take them out in the small boat and putt putted into Minto Flats. They refused to cast into the weeds along the edges of the sloughs where the pike like to lurk, but finally, they caught a small pike that must have managed to get tangled in their line somehow.

They reached camp at midnight and demanded the fish be cooked up for them right then. I dressed and came out of my tent, gutted the fish, seasoned it and wrapped it in tinfoil, tossed it in the coals of the campfire they kept going all the time, told them to turn it in 15 minutes, give it 5 minutes more and eat it. They did.

In the morning, they demanded a return to town as suddenly they decided they needed to go back for the funeral of the lady that died the night before they flew out here. We had no phone contact or radio out here. They got more insulting and obnoxious, they were out of booze.

We heard a plane and it was our pilot, checking on us and taking the fishermen staying in another one of his cabins a bit farther down the slough from where we were staying, back to town. The other fishermen offered to let our 2 jerks fly back in their place and they would go in later as they didn't have a high regard for those two, either.

My Mom and I had gone out to the camp before the men flew in and I had baked a batch of cinnamon rolls to greet them with, when they landed. They wouldn't touch them, but the neighbors sure did and appreciated them, too. Later, the neighbors brought us some buffalo steaks they had from a buffalo they got the year before.

After the plane took off with them, our neighbors offered to let Mom and I stay and cook for them an extra week if we wanted to. We had to decline as we were due back in town in a couple of days. The clients that went in early now wanted a full refund as they didn't stay the entire week. I'm glad most hunters and fishermen are better people than that.

I do like building cabins. So I planned to start on a new project the following spring on 80 acres I purchased about 60 miles northwest of Fairbanks. I wanted to build another underground building. I even drew up plans of sorts, this time. I didn't do that, on the last building project and was told many times that I needed to have plans. I do, they are just in my head.

I had my dozer and backhoe hauled to the new property and built a road in after I got the permit needed for the driveway. I tentatively selected areas that would be nice for building and started clearing so the land had a chance to settle. Next summer we could do some serious building.

We spent the winter planning what to build on the 80 acres. I thought WE were planning, guess only I was, though.

First would be the B&B Aurora viewing Lodge plus work on my underground home. One of the other Assistant Guides I worked with and his wife wanted to join us and build their own. His wife and I chatted daily about the way we wanted to set up the business and how we can have the families involved.

My guy wanted to have the lodge and had contacts for making it a winter destination for aurora viewers from Japan. He took and passed his Registered Guide test also, so that would make two Registered Guides and one Assistant Guide working out of here. They each owned homes in other States and decided to sell up and make this happen. I was thinking everything is going to be wonderful and life would be good again.

My guy was supposed to help out on the payments on the property until my house sold in the spring, as the initial land payments were too high for me to pay on my own. With everyone investing, we would have shared ownership. I could have gone to another bank for the one year financing needed, but he jumped in and said no problem. I can see it was no problem to him, he ignored it. I lived very basic that entire winter, only my Union pension as income and it barely covered the payments and the utilities on the house.

He had promised to be here by April to help pack my house and move everything out. My date to be gone was July 5th. He finally showed up July 3rd. A neighbor at the Homesite, an internet friend from Michigan and a hitchhiker we picked up along the way had packed almost my entire house and helped me haul it to either the Homesite cabin or out to the new property. I started clearing the area I wanted the new underground building to use for guests, storage and workshop areas. It would look a little bit like the starship Enterprise (Star Trek) only mostly underground with open access areas featuring large windows for light inside. I was getting a little disillusioned.

My first cabin (Homesite) was only partially underground in a very steep hill. It is 14 feet into bedrock at the back of the building as I was very afraid of ladders. It was easy to heat in the winter and very cool in the summer. I made extra storage out on the sides that are underground, they don't show from the outside of the building. That is the nicest part of building underground. Who cares if something sticks out?

Besides, out of town that far, there are no building codes. I was experienced now after building on the Homesite and the access road to it while Charlie was still alive. My road building skills improved after building most of "At Your Own Risk Road" that accessed the Homesite to the highway. I got to name the road because I built it.

I learned to operate a roadgrader on that, as I was told if I could start the grader and drive it off, I could have it. Since it took me about 3 hours to find all the shut off switches and how to start it, I finally drove it to the Homesite and was afraid to drop the blade. Lucky for me, it was up when I started the grader.

Charlie got home from work, drove it about 50 feet, operating the levers and pedals, said, "It's all yours", jumped down and left me to it. That was my training. The man wanted the grader back later, so I gave it back.

The Guide I worked for.

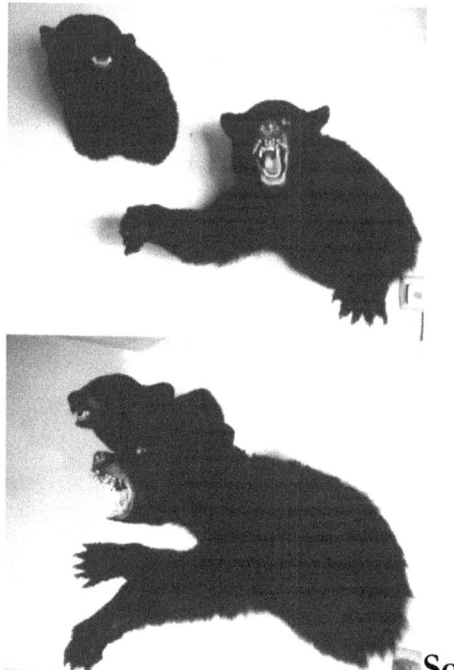

Some of my taxidermy work.

Homesite cabin, dirt bermed, my first building.

Chapter 25

   Okay, another glitch in plans. Boy, was I mixed up on that so-called relationship and as for telling the guy that I loved him? I must have been delusional. Now I don't trust anything I might think I feel for anyone. What a jerk he turned out to be. So, with that said, I will continue.

   The plan to build a bed and breakfast to have income in the winter months for aurora viewing did not materialize. The hunting business also didn't, since it turned out everyone in our group wanted to do it, but I was supposed to foot the entire bill for everything and I had already spent all I had buying the property, paying for my equipment being hauled and all the other expenses to date.

   To really frost the cake, the jerk started covering the cellar built at the underground building, with my backhoe instead of carefully with a wheelbarrow, not being careful to only place sifted loose soil gently over the insulation and vapor barriers. He just dropped buckets of rock and whatever directly on it, then the swing arm pin dropped out and he smacked the corner of the cellar, breaking off the support pole with the back bucket on the backhoe. Totally ruined all the summer's worth of work. That can never be built, now.

Two years later, he finally helped me fix the backhoe as it took 3 hands to hold the pin, adjust the swing arm and tap the pin in place. He needed to use it, so finally helped. He dug out an enormous hole for an outhouse, placed poles across it to cover the area except the center where he built a very small outhouse over the huge hole, then covered the poles with dirt. It has since sloughed in and dropped the outhouse partway down the hole.

Then I found out that he seldom opens letters so never read any of the plans I thought we were agreed on about this place. His assorted girlfriends' letters mostly remain unopened. However, one did send me pictures of their trip to the Tetons. Evidently, he doesn't read long emails, either.

I learned how to build a frame building by building a small guest cabin near the main road. It was quite a learning experience for me. Frame building is a lot different than log building. We had a warm spell in January so my old dozer started, I cleared out a space and used a pick and a grubhoe to make a building pad on the frozen soil. I set pier blocks and used a chainsaw for all the cutting required on boards as there was no source of power.

This was one story with a sleeping loft over 2/3 of the downstairs area, leaving part of it open over the living room area.

I figured out how to build a circular staircase so it wouldn't take up much room and installed it, mostly. The other man that was supposed to have been a partner, only his now ex- wife never told him what we were talking about, moved in before I had it completed. He had spasmodic atrial fibrillation and couldn't work for a living anymore and was now broke. Nowhere to go and no money to live on.

We lived in a single story of what was supposed to be a 2 story house, until my Mom had to move up here for her health. She sent up the money to build her a nice home and the three of us did work on that project for 28 days and got the shell built for a 32 x 40 house. Mom couldn't travel alone now as she had suffered some type of illness that to me mimicked a stroke but her doctor claimed it wasn't. She had memory loss and trouble using one side. Sounds like a stroke, right?

My daughter and I drew straws to see who would fly down to Oregon and accompany her back to Alaska. I cheated. We drew straws alright, but I held the straws, they were all the same length, short, and let her draw first. Yippee, she got the short straw. It was just before Thanksgiving and I was worried my canned goods would freeze up out at the property as I was the one that usually made sure the fire was kept going.

Then the guy living in the guest cabin learned how to do the inside work while on the payroll, while the other one took off on a job somewhere else like he had done ever since he moved up here.

We worked on it every day, insulating and vapor barrier after I drilled into the corners and filled them with foam as they had not been insulated while building. We worked until it looked really good and Mom loved it. The entire downstairs was all finished in varnished wood. Even the interior doors were natural wood and it all had a golden glow that gave it a warm feeling.

The upstairs wasn't finished but we made bookshelves along the outside walls and filled them. Between Mom and me, we have many thousands of books. Mom couldn't live on her own now and my relationship had hit the skids big time with the jerk since I don't like to share. Been there, done that, not doing it again.

His ideal was to have a harem supporting him, he said. He really thought the fellows in Utah that do that are living the perfect life. So I moved Mom and me down to her house and we settled in. Besides, I was getting tired of being told I was fat and stupid since I don't have any college degrees. To be on the job with his crew and have him tell them everyone should have a big fat Alaskan woman, shade in the summer and warm in the winter, really didn't sit well and the crew kept looking at me oddly after that. He said it was just joking, yup.

Then he told everyone I was the smartest dumb person he ever knew, yeah, that went over big time, too. Then he said it was just that I wasn't well educated. Little "jokes" like that get to me after a while. Those three college degrees he has certainly make a difference. If he thinks I am too fat, he doesn't ever have to look at my fat body again. He even told my sister I was too overweight. He made suggestive remarks to everyone, family, friends and neighbors.

I put a little bed upstairs near Mom's entertainment area by my computer corner. We didn't want a TV downstairs, this is out in the woods and there is no TV reception nor cable anyway. We have hundreds of videos and she can pick whatever she wanted to watch each evening while the generator was on, keeping the freezer cold.

My daughters' home she rented from me in town, sold and with my profit, I started building a shop down below my Moms' house on the hill here. We started it in August and my daughter and 3 kids moved into it on October 5th, so it wasn't exactly code or fancy, but it was warm.

We started her a home farther up the hill in June (I had some major surgery the end of April and the Doctor said I could go back to doing my usual activities by mid-June) and had it enclosed and ready for roofing by the end of August. The jerk had volunteered to roof it but kept putting it off until late September as the first snow was falling and then said no, too cold. A neighbor showed up and climbed up, said let's get it done, and they roofed it in a few hours.

Unfortunately, no place was cut or set for a chimney. The chimney jack was sitting right under the framework built in to support it on the roof. Since we couldn't heat it to work on it during the winter, they had to stay another winter in the shop. 1 adult, 3 teenagers, 2 dogs and 8 cats in a 16' x 24' 2 story building.

I had to have repair surgery then, since maybe building a house was not what the doctor had in mind when he said I could go back to my usual activities.

The following summer, we insulated, wired and finished the walls in her house, but still no chimney until late autumn again rolled around. We had found someone not afraid of heights to go out and fix that, when the jerk showed up and did it. What a guy.

As a gift, Mom had satellite internet installed. It only worked when the generator was on and even then, not always very well. Years later, my daughter had a different company install satellite internet on her house and I get mine from her now. This company works much better and we can actually get service when it doesn't.

I built an addition onto Mom's house finally, so I would have a bedroom and space to call my own. It is actually a small efficiency apartment.

One summer, my daughter decided she needed some sort of income since none of our previous plans were happening. A friend gave her an old travel trailer frame. We built a little snack shack on it as they have different regulations than other food service that are not on wheels. It is doing fairly good, considering the "Insurance" signs at the driveway.

I had an outpatient surgery, removing a cyst and went home to recover. Five days later, I almost bled to death from it and my daughter managed to drive me to the hospital in 45 minutes. I got several units of packed red blood cells and a 6 day stay in the hospital. That is the longest I have ever been in a hospital no matter what was wrong. All on a simple outpatient surgical procedure. We did learn that the police are not allowed to run interference using lights and/or siren to get to the hospital any faster.

Mom improved so much since we started some different treatment and stopped some others. Her Oregon doctor had her on a box full of medications, most to counteract other medications. We sorted through, looked up what each one was for and how it was used and slowly weaned her off several until she was only taking 3 a day and she started improving almost immediately. My brother-in-law works in medicine so was able to tell us what each pill was actually supposed to be used for and how to stop taking it. She did have Alzheimer's, though.

We have had a wonderful several years. I was planning on our going for a 4-wheeled ATV ride which she loved, to go to my daughter's for dinner when I found Mom on the couch, sleeping. She napped that way quite often so I didn't think anything about it and made the salad I was to bring as our part of dinner.

Then she vomited, but not even trying to sit up and I knew something was wrong. I cleaned her up and asked if she wanted to go to the doctor, she shook her head NO and started getting agitated. So I helped her into her bedroom and she nodded yes when I asked if she wanted me to bring some dinner home for her.

When I returned, she was on the floor in her bedroom, and could not get up even with assistance. I went back to my daughter's, got her youngest son that was still living at home and he helped me load her into the smaller pickup as it was the easiest for that and we headed for town.

We may have broken a few speed limits and as we crested over the hill by Haglebarger Drive turnoff, there was a State Trooper checking speed. Since they are not allowed to go ahead and use their siren to assist in getting to a hospital faster, I figured one following with siren blazing would do just as well. Grandson asked if we were in trouble and I said I would be, later, but for now, we were going to the hospital as Mom had gotten unresponsive.

Sure enough, the Trooper followed with lights flashing and siren blaring and traffic moved out of our way. At the emergency entrance, he pulled in behind me just as the back door of the little pickup opened and my 6'7" Grandson unfolded from the backseat to go get help. The Troopers eyes kept going up until he was looking into my Grandson's face, but that didn't slow the boy down.

He headed inside and told them to bring a gurney but they brought a wheelchair anyway and he was right behind them with the gurney. I handed the Trooper my license, figuring I may never see it again and handed Mom's information over to the man at the other door of the pickup, that decided the gurney was better.

 Mom vomited almost all blood again as the Trooper started to say something. He looked at us all as the orderlies moved Mom out onto the gurney and headed inside.

He did give me a lecture of safe driving and calling an ambulance, so I tried to explain that there is no phone service out here and by the time we could call, we would be in town anyway. He was very understanding and I wish I had written down his name as he was so helpful after that so I could thank him properly. He said it was obvious my day already wasn't going well, he would not add to it and left, no ticket. A super nice man.

After doing a scan of Mom's head it showed a huge black mass on the right side a bit larger than a tennis ball with swelling mashing the rest of her brain. The doctor told me that even if they could get all the bleeding stopped now that was going on, she would never be more than a vegetable. Certainly not the person she was and she would have hated that.

Mom died after a 5 day stay in the hospital in June, 2011. She had been doing very well, right up until the evening we rushed her in. I miss her.

I have let my Guide license lapse. The State raised the annual fee, almost quadrupling it and added the leasing of a minimum of land for each hunting unit licensed in. This does not mean a person can keep others off the property being leased to hunt on, it does mean that the Guide must pay an annual lease fee just to possibly walk on it and maybe have success for the client that is hunting on it. Everyone else with a hunting license can use it also.

When guiding for myself, I only took family, friends and wanted to start taking wounded veterans out, not paying clients. I only took paying clients out for the Guide I worked for as I didn't want to ever be in competition with him. This made it impossible for me to continue doing that.

When the license was only $100 a year, I could manage that for doing free hunts, but the added price and requirements made it out of my reach. Since the Guide I had been working for was no longer hiring me to work for him, I just dropped the whole thing. I only got it to start with to help him and his family out anyway. Guess it is on to a different career choice now.

It seems I add a new career every decade or so, anyway. I would have liked to continue on this one a bit longer though and quit because I wanted to, not from circumstances.

April 1st one year, a State Trooper pulled in our driveway as I was plowing some snow and said he had to talk to me. Someone had turned me in for baiting moose. Say what?

I laughed, thinking it was an April Fool's joke. He said no, no joke, someone really had called me in for baiting a moose out along the highway, hoping for roadkill by falling a birch tree above the road so the top was in the edge of the highway, right in a curve so any moose feeding on the top would get hit by anyone coming around the corner.

I told him if I wanted to bait moose, I would get one of the ones coming into the yard where it would be a clean kill without mangling the meat. I went out to look and sure enough, someone did one of those slanted cuts to assure the tree would fall in the highway. Who doesn't like me that much? I had a couple of suspicions, but it seems to have stopped since the death of one person. The bullet holes have quit showing up in my road signs, too.

The B&B has never been finished.   Guest cabin

Shop   Mom's house

Daughter's house   Grandson's house

PART SIX – ACCEPTANCE (SORT OF)

Chapter 26

The last few years of Mom's life, my sister and her husband came up every two years and helped out around the place. Major help, not just little dinky things. They are very talented and hard workers.

One spring, we sided the entire house. My little apartment on the back was sided, but the rest was still housewrap over OSB sheets. Firewood was cut and hauled in the morning, then we worked on siding the rest of the day. We used the ladder in the pickup bed to reach the highest parts. It's a good thing this wasn't a job with Inspectors around. Weekends, we did some sightseeing and running around.

Their next trip up, we built a woodshed so I wouldn't have to dig the wood piles out of snow banks all winter. We built an open shed, 10 x 24 feet long beside the driveway. We also filled it. After they left, a friend and I added another 10 x 8 section onto it, then mostly filled it also.

We used peeled poles and logs for the construction and it has held up very well, not like the shed I had built before out of 2x4s that seemed to have more knots in them than strong boards and broke easily, collapsing the entire woodshed on top of the wood stored inside. Then I had to finish out the winter, burrowing under the mess to get wood for the house.

When the EPA didn't renew the waiver for Alaska on the type of diesel/heating oil used in Alaska, the new stuff sooted up our gravity drip oil heaters so badly that they can not be used.

Then, 2 years after the fact, we were told the fuel company should have told us to replace the burner tips on our heaters and we could have continued using oil for auxiliary heat during cold weather. As it is, now we are used to using only wood and are managing quite well at it.

Of course now the EPA is telling everyone they can not burn wood. The oil drip heaters seem to no longer be available. Everyone is supposed to have electricity, I guess. Great, what are people that live out like we do supposed to do?

In my opinion, they are just trying to force everyone to live in the confines of a town or city where they can be more easily controlled. A densely populated area is more easily led than a sparsely populated area. Of course a dense population is more prone to dying off in an epidemic or military attack, also.

I always thought if I wanted to live out beyond the so-called conveniences of life such as electricity, phone service, water and sewer utilities, trash pickup and local mail delivery with a grocery store a few blocks away that I could do so without being considered some sort of oddity.

It seems that society as whole doesn't approve of anyone not conforming to the approved mold. That doesn't say much for society, in my opinion. Of course I don't much care for most of society, either, so it is mutual.

I finally outgrew whatever made me look blue most of my early life. My hands, feet and face usually always had a blue tint to them and the first thing my sister said when she saw me again after we renewed our acquaintance was, "You aren't blue any more." I do have one valve in my heart that flutters instead of closing with each beat, but it has always been that way and probably always will be. My fingernails still get blue once in a while, so does around my lips.

I have a different outlook on life now, than I did before Charlie died. I do more spur of the moment things and do not think I have to pay so much attention to what anyone else is going to think about my actions. I am certainly living more for myself and doing what I want, now. Except for mining. I would like to still be mining. My sluicebox was buried by a neighbor, and my pump was stolen.

This country was founded as a Republic, not a Democracy. It was founded on the belief that a person should be able to keep what he or she has worked for, to improve their lot in life. It was not founded on the principle that everything belongs to "The People". That is Socialism. Socialism is not even working in the Socialist countries, why are people trying to make our country that way? Now with all the illegal migrants flooding in, our Country is getting overrun by them and some of our government is encouraging it.

If I have the courage or stupidity to risk everything I own in an attempt to better my circumstances, which is up to me. I do not want nor need someone telling me not to. It is my risk, let me live with it. Whatever happened to good old hard work, earn it by yourself, for yourself? What happened to being responsible for our own actions? Accountability and consequences, anyone?

Thanks to the internet, I can publish my writing. Publishers want phone access or at least easy postal service access. I have neither. I pick and choose which portions of civilization I wish to accommodate.

I love the peace and quiet out here, watching the wildlife and getting out of the way of some of it. We observe but seldom interfere.

My daughter has 3 kids, two sons and a daughter. Her oldest son has a son, also, that he has full custody of and has raised. Her Daughter has 2 children, a boy and a girl. My son has 5 children, three boys and twin daughters.

My oldest stepdaughter remarried and lives near North Pole, Alaska. She has 2 kids, a son and a daughter. Other stepdaughter has 2 kids, also a son and a daughter and lives in Hawaii. I have lost track of the other two boys.

I really enjoy grandchildren, can always tell them to go home, their folks want them.

Did you know that if you hit the panic button on your keychain, you actually can panic a bear that is getting too close in your yard? I didn't either. I wish we had video of that one.

My father, 1918   My mother, 1941

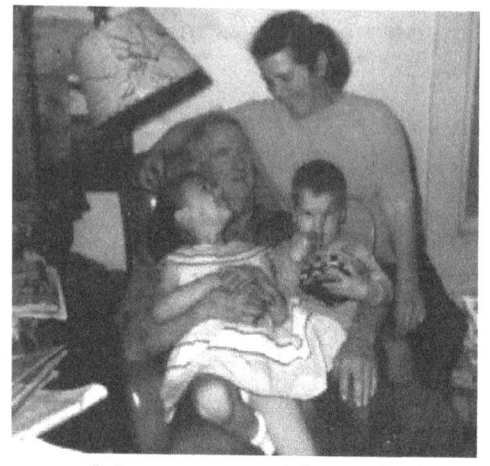
My parents with my kids.

The man we stayed with, while hunting

A lampblack painting I did

Mom and I with my 2nd moose

My 1st Bear hunt client

My 1st moose hunting client

Me, oldest grandson and my Mom at that old cabin. We scattered Charlie's Ashes on top the hill.

No meat wasted, shoot their heads off, this was right after I scorched most of my hair off. New hair style.

Me doing laundry   Downhill from Mom's house the greenhouse, garden and shop.

Five Generations. My Mom, my daughter and her three kids and grandson, plus my sister and her husband oh yeah, me, too.

My daughter's Hit & Run Snack Shack, using some of my artwork for her logo.

We are well insured

A couple of the dolls I made

Another of my lampblack paintings

Oil paints on a beaver pelt

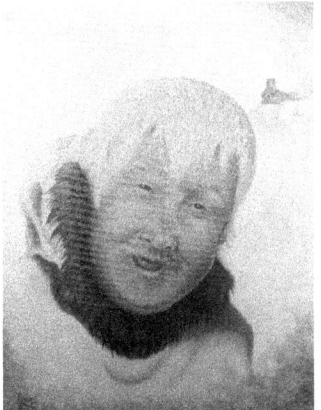

Oil paint on canvas

My favorite toy, a gift from Charlie. No one else operates it, if it broke, I would hurt them.

Me, 1 week before my 70th birthday

This is a totally biased opinionated version of my life, told strictly from my point of view. If I have offended anyone, too bad, get over it. .

Not quite the end.

www.ingramcontent.com/pod-product-compliance
Lightning Source LLC
Chambersburg PA
CBHW071110160426
43196CB00013B/2527